# Knitting Stitches Demystified

## Your Ultimate Guidebook for Effortless Learning

**Titusa K Ina**

# THIS BOOK

**BELONGS TO**

.................................................................

.................................................................

I can't tell you how grateful I am that you decided to read my book. My most heartfelt thanks that you took time out of your life to choose my work and I hope you find benefit within these pages.

There are so many books available today that offer similar content so that makes it even more humbling that you decided to buying mine.

Tell me what you thought! I am eager to hear your opinion and ideas on what you read as are others who are looking for a good book to buy. Leave a review on Amazon.com so others can benefit from your wisdom!

***With much thanks.***

# Table of Contents

SUMMARY                                                          1

Introduction                                                    27

Why Hand Knitting                                               28

Some Facts about Knitting                                       29

The Right Tools and Materials                                   30

Yarn for Beginners                                              32

Needles for Beginners                                           44

A Journal for Knitting                                          54

Other Necessary Tools                                           55

Getting Started with Patterns                                   57

Pattern Basics                                                  58

Standard Abbreviations for Knitting Patterns                    60

How to Read a Pattern                                           66

How to Hold the Needles and Yarn                                67

Stitches                                                        71

Casting On Stitches                                             72

The Basic Bind-Off                                              79

The Knit Stitch                                                 82

The Purl Stitch                                                 86

The Garter Stitch                                               89

The Stockinette Stitch                                          95

Basic Ribbing                                                  101

Seed Stitch                                                    105

Double Seed Stitch                                             111

Roman Stitch                                                   118

The Linen Stitch                                               121

Cable and Twist Stitches                                       125

The Bobble Stitch                                              133

Techniques                                                     144

Eyelets and Lace Stitches                                      145

Zigzag Stitch                                                  151

Slipping Stitch                                                157

Drop Stitch                          159

Multi-Colored Stitch                 164

Leaf Stitches-Lace                   167

Border & Edging Stitches             175

Rounded Patterns                     178

Geometric Patterns                   185

Knit Circular or Flat                188

Patterns                             190

Stich Scarf                          191

Leaves Jacket                        193

Snowy Owl                            201

Common Mistakes in Knitting          210

Dropping a Stitch                    210

Too Many Stitches                    211

Tight Knitting                       214

FAQ                                  215

Conclusion                           220

# SUMMARY

**What is The Knitting**: The Knitting is a popular and versatile craft that involves creating fabric by interlocking loops of yarn or thread using knitting needles or a knitting machine. It is a technique that has been practiced for centuries and has evolved over time to become a beloved hobby for many people around the world.

The process of knitting involves manipulating the yarn or thread with the knitting needles to create various stitches, which are then combined to form a pattern or design. The basic stitches in knitting include the knit stitch and the purl stitch, which are used to create different textures and patterns in the fabric. By combining these stitches in different ways, knitters can create a wide range of items, from simple scarves and hats to intricate sweaters and blankets.

One of the great things about knitting is its versatility. It can be done with a wide variety of materials, including different types of yarn, thread, and even wire. This allows knitters to experiment with different textures, colors, and thicknesses to create unique and personalized pieces. Additionally, knitting can be done by people of all ages and skill levels, making it a great activity for both beginners and experienced crafters.

Knitting is not only a creative outlet, but it also offers numerous benefits for the knitter. It is a relaxing and meditative activity that can help reduce stress and anxiety. The repetitive motions of knitting can have a calming effect on the mind and body, similar to other forms of mindfulness practices. Knitting can also improve hand-eye coordination and fine motor skills, as it requires precise movements and control of the knitting needles.

Furthermore, knitting allows for self-expression and individuality. With countless patterns and designs available, knitters can choose to follow a pattern or create their own unique designs. This allows for a sense of accomplishment and pride in the finished product. Knitting can also be a social activity, as many people enjoy knitting in groups or attending knitting circles where they can share tips, patterns, and stories with fellow knitters.

In addition to being a hobby, knitting has a rich history and cultural significance. It has been practiced by various cultures around the world for centuries, with each culture adding its own unique techniques and styles to the craft. Knitted garments have been worn for warmth and protection throughout history, and knitting has also been used as a form of artistic expression and storytelling.

In conclusion, knitting is a versatile and enjoyable craft that offers numerous benefits for the knitter.

**The Impact and Importance of Mastering Knitting Stitches**: Knitting is a craft that has been practiced for centuries, and mastering knitting stitches is essential for anyone who wants to become proficient in this art form. The impact and importance of mastering knitting stitches cannot be overstated, as it is the foundation upon which all knitting projects are built.

One of the key reasons why mastering knitting stitches is important is that it allows knitters to create a wide variety of patterns and designs. Each stitch has its own unique characteristics and creates a different texture and appearance in the finished piece. By mastering a range of stitches, knitters can create intricate lace patterns, cozy cables, and beautiful colorwork. The possibilities are endless, and the ability to combine different stitches opens up a world of creativity and artistic expression.

Furthermore, mastering knitting stitches is crucial for achieving a professional and polished finish in knitting projects. When stitches are executed correctly, the fabric is even and smooth, with no loose or uneven stitches. This attention to detail is what sets apart a well-made knitted item from a poorly executed one. By mastering knitting stitches, knitters can ensure that their finished projects have a high-quality and professional appearance.

In addition to the aesthetic benefits, mastering knitting stitches also improves the efficiency and speed of knitting. When knitters are familiar with the different stitches and techniques, they can work more quickly and with greater ease. This allows them to complete projects in a timely manner and take on more complex and challenging patterns. It also reduces the likelihood of making mistakes or having to constantly refer to instructions, as the stitches become second nature.

Moreover, mastering knitting stitches enhances problem-solving skills and fosters a sense of accomplishment. Knitting is not always straightforward, and knitters often encounter challenges and obstacles along the way. By understanding the mechanics of different stitches, knitters can troubleshoot and find solutions to common knitting problems, such as dropped stitches or twisted cables. This ability to problem-solve and overcome obstacles builds resilience and confidence, and knitters feel a sense of pride and satisfaction when they successfully navigate through difficult patterns.

Lastly, mastering knitting stitches allows for the preservation and continuation of a traditional craft. Knitting has a rich history and cultural significance, and by mastering the stitches, knitters contribute to the preservation of this heritage. They become part of a community of knitters who share a passion for the craft and can pass on their knowledge and skills to future generations.

In conclusion, mastering knitting stitches is of utmost importance for anyone who wants to excel in the art of knitting.

**The Fundamentals of Knitting**: The Fundamentals of Knitting is a comprehensive guide that covers all the essential aspects of this popular craft. Whether you are a beginner or an experienced knitter looking to enhance your skills, this book is a valuable resource that will help you master the art of knitting.

The book starts with an introduction to the history of knitting, tracing its origins back to ancient times and highlighting its evolution over the years. This section provides a fascinating insight into the cultural significance of knitting and how it has been passed down through generations.

Next, the book delves into the basic tools and materials needed for knitting. It explains the different types of knitting needles, yarns, and other accessories that are essential for any knitting project. The author provides detailed explanations and recommendations, making it easy for readers to understand and choose the right tools for their needs.

The following chapters focus on the fundamental techniques of knitting. Starting with the basic knit and purl stitches, the book gradually introduces more advanced techniques such as increasing, decreasing, and shaping. Each technique is explained in a step-by-step manner, accompanied by clear illustrations and photographs that make it easy to follow along.

As the book progresses, it covers a wide range of knitting patterns and projects. From simple scarves and hats to intricate sweaters and blankets, the author provides a variety of patterns that cater to different skill levels. Each pattern is accompanied by detailed instructions, including stitch counts, gauge measurements, and finishing techniques, ensuring that readers can successfully complete their projects.

In addition to the technical aspects of knitting, the book also explores the creative side of this craft. It discusses color theory, pattern design, and different knitting styles, encouraging readers to experiment and personalize their projects. The author also shares tips and tricks for troubleshooting common knitting problems, ensuring that readers can overcome any challenges they may encounter.

The Fundamentals of Knitting goes beyond just teaching the techniques and patterns. It also emphasizes the therapeutic and meditative aspects of knitting, highlighting its ability to reduce stress and promote mindfulness. The book includes anecdotes and stories from knitters around the world, showcasing the sense of community and connection that knitting can foster.

Overall, The Fundamentals of Knitting is a comprehensive guide that covers everything you need to know about knitting. Whether you are a beginner or an experienced knitter, this book will equip you with the knowledge and skills to create beautiful and unique knitted items. With its detailed instructions, helpful tips, and inspiring stories, this book is a must-have for anyone interested in

**Introduction to Yarn, Needles, and Basic Tools of Knitting**:

Knitting is a popular craft that involves creating fabric by interlocking loops of yarn with the use of knitting needles. It is a versatile and creative hobby that allows individuals to make a wide range of items, from cozy sweaters and scarves to intricate lace patterns and blankets. To get started with knitting, it is essential to have a good understanding of the basic tools involved, including yarn and needles.

Yarn is the primary material used in knitting and comes in a variety of fibers, weights, and colors. The choice of yarn can greatly impact the final outcome of a project, so it is important to select the right type for your desired project. Common yarn fibers include wool, cotton, acrylic, and blends of different materials. Each fiber has its own unique characteristics, such as warmth, softness, and durability. The weight of the yarn refers to its thickness, which can range from super fine to super bulky. Thinner yarns are typically used for delicate projects, while thicker yarns are ideal for creating chunky and cozy items. Additionally, yarns come in a wide array of colors and patterns, allowing knitters to unleash their creativity and personalize their projects.

Knitting needles are the tools used to create the loops in the yarn. They come in various materials, such as metal, wood, and plastic, each offering different benefits. Metal needles are known for their smoothness and durability, while wooden needles provide a warm and comfortable grip. Plastic needles are lightweight and often preferred by beginners due to their affordability. The size of the needles is determined by their diameter, which is measured in millimeters or US sizes. The size of the needles should correspond to the weight of the yarn being used, as indicated on the yarn label. Thinner needles are used with finer yarns, while thicker needles are used with bulkier yarns. It is important to choose the right needle size to achieve the desired tension and gauge in your knitting.

In addition to yarn and needles, there are a few basic tools that every knitter should have. These include a pair of scissors for cutting yarn, a tapestry needle for weaving in loose ends, stitch markers to keep track of pattern repeats, and a measuring tape for checking gauge and sizing. These tools are essential for completing knitting projects efficiently and with precision.

In conclusion, knitting is a rewarding and enjoyable craft that requires a good understanding of the basic tools involved.

**Understanding Yarn Weights and Needle Sizes of Knitting:**

When it comes to knitting, understanding yarn weights and needle sizes is essential for achieving the desired outcome of your project. Yarn weight refers to the thickness or thickness of the yarn, while needle size determines the size of the stitches and the overall tension of your knitting.

Yarn weight is typically categorized into several different categories, ranging from lace weight to super bulky. Each weight category has its own characteristics and is suitable for different types of projects. Lace weight yarn is the thinnest and is often used for delicate and intricate lace patterns. Fingering weight yarn is slightly thicker and is commonly used for lightweight garments and accessories. Sport weight yarn is a bit thicker and is suitable for baby items and lightweight sweaters. Worsted weight yarn is one of the most popular choices and is versatile enough for a wide range of projects, including scarves, hats, and blankets. Bulky and super bulky yarns are much thicker and are perfect for cozy winter accessories and chunky blankets.

In addition to yarn weight, needle size also plays a crucial role in knitting. The size of the needles you use will determine the size of the stitches and the overall tension of your knitting. Needle sizes are typically measured in millimeters or US sizes. The smaller the needle size, the smaller the stitches will be, resulting in a tighter and denser fabric. Conversely, larger needle sizes will create larger stitches and a looser fabric. It's important to choose the right needle size for your yarn weight to ensure that your stitches are even and your finished project turns out as intended.

To determine the appropriate needle size for your yarn, you can refer to the yarn label or consult a knitting pattern. Yarn labels often provide a recommended needle size range for that particular yarn. Knitting patterns will also specify the recommended needle size to achieve the desired gauge, which is the number of stitches and rows per inch. Achieving the correct gauge is crucial for ensuring that your finished project matches the measurements and fit specified in the pattern.

It's worth noting that needle size can also affect the drape and texture of your knitted fabric. Using smaller needles will create a denser fabric with less drape, while larger needles will result in a looser fabric with more drape. This is an important consideration when choosing needle size for different types of projects.

**Setting Up: Making a Slipknot and Casting On of Knitting**:

Knitting is a popular craft that involves creating fabric by interlocking loops of yarn with knitting needles. Before you can start knitting, you need to set up your project by making a slipknot and casting on. These initial steps are crucial as they determine the number of stitches you will have on your needle and the foundation of your knitting project.

To begin, you will need a ball of yarn and a pair of knitting needles. Choose a yarn that suits your project, considering factors such as color, weight, and fiber content. Thicker yarns are ideal for chunky knits, while finer yarns are better for delicate projects. Once you have your yarn and needles ready, you can proceed to make a slipknot.

A slipknot is a loop that can be easily adjusted and tightened. It serves as the first stitch on your needle and provides a starting point for your knitting. To make a slipknot, hold the end of the yarn in your dominant hand and create a loop by crossing the yarn over itself. Insert your fingers through the loop and grab the working end of the yarn. Pull the working end through the loop, creating a slipknot. Adjust the loop's size by pulling the working end or the tail of the yarn until it fits comfortably on your needle.

Once you have your slipknot ready, it's time to cast on. Casting on is the process of creating the foundation row of stitches on your needle. There are various methods for casting on, but the most common one is the long-tail cast on. This method creates a neat and elastic edge, making it suitable for a wide range of knitting projects.

To perform the long-tail cast on, hold the needle with the slipknot in your non-dominant hand. With your dominant hand, hold the working end of the yarn and the tail together, leaving a tail that is approximately three times the width of your desired knitting project. Place your thumb and index finger between the two strands of yarn, creating a "V" shape.

Insert the needle into the "V" shape from front to back, catching the working end of the yarn with the needle. Bring the needle under the tail of the yarn and then over the working end, creating a loop on the needle. Slide this loop onto the needle, tightening it slightly.

**The Knit Stitch: Techniques and Tips of Knitting:** This is a comprehensive guide that delves into the intricacies of the knit stitch, providing readers with a wealth of knowledge and practical tips to enhance their knitting skills. Whether you are a beginner or an experienced knitter, this book is designed to cater to all levels of expertise.

The book begins by introducing the fundamental concepts of knitting, explaining the basic tools and materials required for the craft. It covers the different types of knitting needles, yarns, and other accessories, providing readers with a solid foundation to embark on their knitting journey.

Moving on, the book delves into the core technique of knitting - the knit stitch. It breaks down the stitch into its various components, explaining each step in detail. From casting on to binding off, every aspect of the knit stitch is thoroughly explored, ensuring that readers have a comprehensive understanding of the technique.

One of the standout features of this book is its emphasis on technique. The author goes beyond simply explaining how to execute the knit stitch; they delve into the nuances of tension, gauge, and stitch formation. By understanding these finer points, readers can achieve more professional-looking results and overcome common knitting challenges.

In addition to technique, "The Knit Stitch" also provides readers with a plethora of tips and tricks to enhance their knitting experience. From troubleshooting common mistakes to mastering advanced techniques, the book covers a wide range of topics that will undoubtedly benefit knitters of all skill levels.

Furthermore, the book includes a variety of knitting patterns that allow readers to put their newfound skills to use. These patterns range from simple projects suitable for beginners to more complex designs for advanced knitters. Each pattern is accompanied by clear instructions and detailed diagrams, making it easy for readers to follow along and create beautiful knitted items.

it is a comprehensive resource that will become an invaluable companion for any knitting enthusiast. With its detailed explanations, practical tips, and inspiring patterns, this book is sure to ignite a passion for knitting and empower readers to take their skills to new heights. Whether you are looking to learn the basics or expand your knitting repertoire, this book is a must-have for every knitter's library."

This is a comprehensive guide that delves into the intricacies of the purl stitch, a fundamental technique in the art of knitting. This book is a must-have for both beginners and experienced knitters who are looking to enhance their skills and expand their repertoire.

The author takes a systematic approach to teaching the purl stitch, breaking it down into its basic components and explaining each step in a clear and concise manner. The book begins with an introduction to the purl stitch, providing a brief history of its origins and its significance in knitting. It then progresses to the various methods of executing the stitch, including the English method, the Continental method, and the combination method. Each method is explained in detail, with step-by-step instructions and accompanying illustrations to ensure a thorough understanding.

One of the standout features of this book is its emphasis on mastery. The author not only teaches the reader how to perform the purl stitch, but also provides valuable tips and techniques for achieving precision and consistency. From tension control to stitch formation, the author covers all aspects of mastering the purl stitch, ensuring that the reader develops a strong foundation in this essential knitting technique.

In addition to the technical aspects, this book also explores the creative possibilities of the purl stitch. The author showcases various stitch patterns and designs that can be achieved using the purl stitch, inspiring knitters to experiment and create their own unique projects. Whether it's a textured scarf, a cozy sweater, or an intricate lace shawl, this book provides the tools and knowledge needed to bring any knitting project to life.

Furthermore, the book includes troubleshooting tips and common mistakes to avoid, ensuring that knitters can overcome any challenges they may encounter while working with the purl stitch. The author's expertise and experience shine through in these sections, offering invaluable guidance and support to knitters of all levels.

This book is not just a book, but a comprehensive resource that will become an indispensable companion for any knitter. With its detailed instructions, helpful illustrations, and insightful tips, this book equips readers with the skills and knowledge needed to become proficient in the purl stitch and take their knitting to new heights. Whether you're a beginner looking to learn the basics or an experienced knitter seeking to refine your technique, this book is a must-read.

**Combining Knit and Purl Stitches:** Combining knit and purl stitches is a fundamental technique in knitting that allows for the creation of various patterns and textures in your knitted fabric. By alternating between these two basic stitches, you can achieve a wide range of designs, from simple ribbing to intricate cables.

To combine knit and purl stitches, you first need to understand the difference between the two. A knit stitch is created by inserting the right-hand needle into the front of the stitch on the left-hand needle, wrapping the yarn around the right-hand needle, and pulling it through the stitch to create a new loop. This results in a smooth, V-shaped stitch on the right side of the fabric. On the other hand, a purl stitch is made by inserting the right-hand needle into the back of the stitch on the left-hand needle, wrapping the yarn around the right-hand needle, and pulling it through the stitch to create a new loop. This creates a bump or purl on the right side of the fabric.

To combine these two stitches, you can create various patterns by alternating between knitting and purling stitches in a specific sequence. One of the most common patterns is ribbing, which is often used for cuffs, collars, and hems. Ribbing is created by alternating knit and purl stitches in a 1x1 or 2x2 pattern. For a 1x1 rib, you knit one stitch and purl one stitch, repeating this sequence across the row. This creates a stretchy and textured fabric that is commonly seen in sweaters and socks. A 2x2 rib is created by knitting two stitches and purling two stitches, repeating this sequence across the row. This pattern is often used for scarves and hats.

Another popular pattern that combines knit and purl stitches is the seed stitch. The seed stitch is created by alternating knit and purl stitches in a 1x1 pattern, but with the stitches reversed on each row. This means that if you knit a stitch on one row, you purl it on the next row, and vice versa. This creates a bumpy texture that resembles a field of seeds, hence the name. The seed stitch is commonly used for blankets, dishcloths, and baby garments.

In addition to ribbing and the seed stitch, you can also combine knit and purl stitches to create more complex patterns, such as cables and lace.

**The Magic of Stripes: Simple Colorwork of Knitting**: this is a comprehensive guide that delves into the fascinating world of colorwork in knitting. This book is a must-have for both beginners and experienced knitters who are looking to add a touch of creativity and visual interest to their projects.

The author takes the reader on a journey through the various techniques and methods used to create stunning striped patterns in knitting. From basic two-color stripes to more intricate designs, this book covers it all. The step-by-step instructions are accompanied by clear and detailed illustrations, making it easy for knitters of all skill levels to follow along.

One of the highlights of this book is the emphasis on simplicity. The author understands that not everyone has the time or patience to tackle complex colorwork projects, so they have included a range of easy-to-follow patterns that yield impressive results. These patterns are perfect for beginners who are just starting to explore the world of colorwork, as well as experienced knitters who are looking for quick and satisfying projects.

In addition to the practical aspects of colorwork knitting, "The Magic of Stripes also delves into the theory behind color combinations and how to choose the perfect palette for your projects. The author provides valuable insights into color theory, helping knitters understand how different hues and shades interact with each other. This knowledge is invaluable when it comes to creating harmonious and visually appealing striped patterns.

Furthermore, the book includes a section on troubleshooting common issues that knitters may encounter while working on colorwork projects. From managing tension to fixing mistakes, the author provides practical tips and tricks to ensure a smooth and enjoyable knitting experience.

The Magic of Stripes is not just a technical guide; it is also a source of inspiration. The book showcases a wide range of finished projects, from cozy scarves and hats to intricate sweaters and blankets. Each project is accompanied by stunning photographs that highlight the beauty and versatility of colorwork knitting.

Overall, This book is a comprehensive and accessible guide that will inspire and empower knitters to explore the world of colorwork. Whether you are a beginner or an experienced knitter, this book is sure to become a valuable resource in your knitting library. So grab your needles and yarn, and let the magic of stripes transform your knitting projects into works of art.

**Exploring Intarsia and Mosaic Knitting**: Intarsia and mosaic knitting are two popular techniques in the world of knitting that allow for the creation of intricate and visually stunning designs. These techniques involve the use of multiple colors and the careful placement of stitches to create patterns and images within the knitted fabric.

Intarsia knitting is a technique that involves knitting with blocks of color. Unlike stranded knitting, where multiple colors are carried along the back of the work, intarsia knitting requires separate balls or bobbins of yarn for each color block. This allows for clean color changes and the creation of large, solid areas of color. Intarsia knitting is often used to create bold geometric designs or to depict images such as animals or flowers.

Mosaic knitting, on the other hand, is a technique that creates the illusion of complex colorwork using only one color per row. This is achieved by slipping stitches and working with a combination of knit and purl stitches. Mosaic knitting is known for its simplicity and the stunning results it can produce. It is often used to create intricate patterns and motifs, such as geometric shapes or floral designs.

Both intarsia and mosaic knitting require careful attention to detail and the ability to read and follow charts or patterns. These techniques can be challenging for beginners, but with practice and patience, they can be mastered. It is important to have a good understanding of basic knitting techniques, such as casting on, knitting, purling, and decreasing, before attempting these more advanced techniques.

When working with intarsia or mosaic knitting, it is important to choose the right yarn and needles for your project. The yarn should be of a similar weight and fiber content for each color block to ensure even tension and a cohesive finished piece. The needles should be the appropriate size for your chosen yarn to achieve the desired gauge.

One of the advantages of intarsia and mosaic knitting is the ability to create unique and personalized projects. By choosing your own colors and patterns, you can create one-of-a-kind garments, accessories, or home decor items. These techniques also offer endless possibilities for creativity and experimentation, allowing you to push the boundaries of traditional knitting and create truly innovative designs.

In conclusion, intarsia and mosaic knitting are two exciting techniques that allow knitters to explore their creativity and create stunning, intricate designs. While they may require some practice and patience, the results are well worth the effort.

**Basic Brioche Stitch Techniques of Knitting:** The basic brioche stitch is a popular knitting technique that creates a unique and textured fabric. It is known for its squishy and reversible nature, making it a great choice for a variety of projects such as scarves, hats, and sweaters. In this article, we will explore the various techniques involved in knitting the basic brioche stitch and provide detailed instructions to help you master this beautiful stitch.

To begin, you will need a pair of knitting needles and two contrasting colors of yarn. The brioche stitch is typically worked with a larger needle size than what is recommended for the yarn to create a looser and more drapey fabric. However, this can vary depending on your personal preference and the desired outcome of your project.

The basic brioche stitch is worked over an even number of stitches. To start, cast on your desired number of stitches using one color of yarn. For example, if you want to cast on 20 stitches, you will have 10 stitches in each color. Once you have cast on, you will work the setup row, which is the foundation for the brioche stitch pattern.

The setup row is worked as follows: *Knit 1, yarn over (yo), slip 1 purlwise with yarn in front (sl1yo)*. Repeat this sequence across the row until you reach the end. This setup row creates the foundation for the brioche stitch pattern and sets up the alternating knit and purl stitches.

After completing the setup row, you will begin working the main rows of the brioche stitch pattern. The main rows are worked in two steps: the first step is called the "brioche knit" and the second step is called the "brioche purl".

To work the brioche knit, insert your right needle into the next stitch as if to knit, but instead of knitting it, you will slip the stitch off the left needle and let it drop. This creates a yarn over (yo) on the right needle. Repeat this step across the row, slipping each stitch off the left needle and creating a yarn over.

Once you have completed the brioche knit row, you will move on to the brioche purl row. To work the brioche purl, bring the yarn to the front of your work and insert your right needle into the next stitch as if to purl.

**Fundamentals of Entrelac Knitting**: The fundamentals of entrelac knitting are a fascinating and intricate technique that allows knitters to create beautiful and unique patterns. Entrelac knitting is characterized by its interlocking diamond shapes, which give the finished piece a three-dimensional appearance.

To begin learning entrelac knitting, it is important to have a solid understanding of basic knitting techniques such as casting on, knitting, purling, and binding off. These skills will serve as the foundation for creating the individual squares that make up the entrelac pattern.

The first step in entrelac knitting is to cast on a multiple of eight stitches. This will ensure that the pattern is symmetrical and balanced. Once the desired number of stitches is cast on, the next step is to work the base triangles. These triangles are created by knitting or purling a set number of stitches, then turning the work and working back in the opposite direction. This process is repeated until the desired number of triangles is achieved.

After completing the base triangles, the next step is to work the side triangles. These triangles are created by picking up stitches along the edges of the base triangles and working them in the same manner as the base triangles. The number of stitches picked up will depend on the desired size and shape of the finished piece.

Once the side triangles are complete, the next step is to work the center squares. These squares are created by picking up stitches along the edges of the side triangles and working them in the same manner as the base triangles. The number of stitches picked up will depend on the desired size and shape of the finished piece.

As the entrelac pattern progresses, the squares and triangles are worked in a continuous manner, with each new section being picked up from the previous section. This creates a seamless and cohesive design.

One of the key aspects of entrelac knitting is the use of short rows. Short rows are used to shape the individual sections of the pattern, allowing for the creation of the distinctive diamond shapes. By working partial rows and turning the work before reaching the end of the row, the knitter can create the necessary angles and curves to form the entrelac pattern.

In addition to the basic techniques, there are also various stitch patterns and colorwork options that can be incorporated into entrelac knitting. This allows for endless possibilities in terms of design and creativity.

# Introduction

**Would you be interested in learning how to knit a wide range of stitches?**

Knitting is a brilliantly useful skill that can help you create a wide variety of your own products – everything from toys to clothing. But, not only that, it's scientifically proven to improve your mood, mind and body. It's a therapeutic skill which you will not regret learning!

This book will teach you the **_knitting basics with step-by-step instructions_** to give you **_all the tools you will need_** to get started. Note that this is not the typical knitting tutorial and every step is quite detailed and abbreviations are explained. Once you have mastered the skills listed within this guide, **you will be able to create anything you desire**, even something unique that is your very own design.

With **close to thirty patterns and clear instructions**, this guide is perfect for newbie knitters who want to build their confidence and skills in knitting and at the same time, it will be a treat for knitters who enjoy modern knitting and simplified details.

This book covers the stitches you need to get started; it explains the best way to read pattern instructions and even gives you a few projects for you to practice your new found skills. There is literally everything you need to learn this craft that will change your life for the better!

# Why Hand Knitting?

The benefits of taking up hand knitting as a hobby are endless. It's a worthwhile pursuit that fills you with the powerful ability to create something beautiful from scratch from yarn, needles and your bare hands, and once you have mastered knitting patterns you can go on to create your own – designing something that is entirely yours. The satisfaction that you'll derive from this expression of creativity will be worth all of the perseverance.

Indeed, knitting is a fun-filled activity. Once you become familiar with what you need to knit, then you can knit anything without using a pattern. This then makes knitting a project that is ideal, especially when travelling. In case you are not driving, knitting is a productive activity that you can engage in before you arrive at your destination, when on a queue or even in a doctor's waiting room. In addition to the above, the other reason why hand knitting is preferred is that once you begin wearing hand knit items, you will easily prefer them over manufactured knitted items that are bought in shops.

*Watch this video explaining [the benefits of knitting](#).*

# Some Facts about Knitting

- There are 7.2 million knitters in the UK alone.

- The UK hobby craft and textile industry estimated to be worth over 3.5billion pounds.

- There is 12% increase in people participating in crafts year after year.

- There are 448,000 men in the UK that have an interest in knitting and sewing.

- Google reports a 70% increase over the last year in searches for 'knitting and crochet' and 250% increase for 'knitting for beginners' over past 5 years which just proves how popular it is becoming as a hobby!

- Ravelry (a Facebook group for knitters) had over 3 million members worldwide in March 2013 and of Ravelry's top 10 most popular yarns, 5 are pure wool, 2 have high wool content, 2 are natural fibres mix, only one is acrylic.

- There are currently 14 mainstream knitting and crochet print magazines with many more available online.

- Knitting and crocheting has been proved to have therapeutic effects by reducing stress, relieving the symptoms of arthritis and giving a general feeling of wellbeing from a sense of achievement. Exeter University has just secured funding for research into this phenomenon.

- Current most popular yarns are wool rich yarns.

- Current most popular knitting project is lace weight shawls.

# The Right Tools and Materials

In order to get started, you will require few basic tools.

As a beginning knitter, one can be tempted buy many things from the knitting store, beautiful needles, fancy yarns, you name it. However, it is only sensible to just buy few supplies when you are beginning to knit. To start with, you are not even sure that you will like knitting and secondly you may just be wasting money on items that you may not even end up using.

You don't really require lots of expensive supplies or even fancy yarns to do your first knitting project. You'll just need something basic and easy to work with as you master all of the skills necessary.

***Just be sure that you have the following:***

- Yarn

- Needles

- Scissors

- A sewing needle

- A crochet hook

*Watch this video for basic knitting supplies*

# Yarn for Beginners

One of the major reasons why people become interested in knitting is that they are attracted to the variety of yarns available. There are many beautiful colors and textures on offer, but you'll want to be careful to select one that suits the pattern you're working on.

You will want to *take the following into consideration*:

- Yarn weight

- Yarn quality

- The color or pattern of the yarn

- Yarn fiber.

# How to Choose Your Yarn

Having identified what you would like to knit for your project, a visit to the yarn store or crafts shop will expose you to a multitude of various types of yarns. Be sure to go armed with the information about what you need, and then touch the different yarns available in order to identify what looks and feels good to wear and work with.

*Watch this video on how to choose knitting yarn.*

When you walk into a craft store or yarn shop, it is quite easy to get overwhelmed by all the different sorts of yarn available. The question is which is the right yarn for your project? You therefore need to know the weight of the yarn.

# Standard Yarn Weight System

Yarn weight refers to the **thickness of the yarn**, which can range from *fine* all the way to *super bulky*.

According to the *Craft Yarn Council of America*, there are in fact six categories of yarn weights. This guide has been set up to demonstrate the ***predicted number of stitches that will be created depending on the needle size you use with the different types of yarn***. It follows that the higher the number is, the heavier the yarn will be and additionally, the fewer the stitches will be per inch.

# Why do Standards Matter

**These standards** are useful because they **help you match your yarn to your pattern**. If it is known with certainty that every bulk yarn will give almost a similar number of stitches, (say 12 to 15 stitches for 4" on the 9 to 11 needle size) and as you choose to work on a pattern, that uses size 10 needles, then you know that you can choose any bulky yarn you wish and it'll work.

It is quite **important that you** endeavor to **knit a gauge swatch to test the yarn and needle sizes, before embarking on a project that involves size**. This is due to the fact that all yarns of a specific weight are almost the same. If trying to make a fit for a sweater, a difference in 12 stitches for every four inches and 15 stitches is quite huge.

*Watch this video on how to knit a gauge swatch.*

# How to Determine Yarn Weight

Most of the manufacturers of yarn make it easy to determine the weight as they print all of the information on the label. Although this sometimes varies from company to company, they will have a gauge statement to assist you. For example, '*24 stitches together with 22 rows for every four stitches on the needle size 4*'.

Below is the chart set by the *Craft Council of America* to help you **determine yarn weights** and **which knitting and crochet needles they will work with**.

| Yarn Weight: | 0 Lace | 1 Super Fine | 2 Fine | 3 Light | 4 Medium | 5 Bulky | 6 Super Bulky |
|---|---|---|---|---|---|---|---|
| Types of Yarn in Category. | Thread, Cobweb, Lace. | Sock, Baby. | Sport, Baby. | DK, Light, Worsted. | Worsted, Afghan. | Chunky, Craft, Rug. | Bulky, Roving. |
| Knit Gauge Range in Stockinet Stitch to 4 inches. | 30 – 40 sts | 27 – 32 sts | 23 – 26 sts | 21 – 24 sts | 16 – 20 sts | 12 – 15 sts | 6 – 11 sts |
| Recommended Needle in Metric Size Range. | 1.5 – 2.25mm | 2.25 – 3.25mm | 3.25 – 3.75mm | 3.75 – 4.5mm | 4.5 – 5.5mm | 5.5 – 8mm | 8mm and larger |
| Recommended Needle in US Size Range. | 000 - 1 | 1 – 3 | 3 – 5 | 5 – 7 | 7 - 9 | 9 - 11 | 11 and more |
| Crochet Gauge Ranges in Single Crochet to 4 inch. | 32 – 42 double crochets | 21 – 32 sts | 16 – 20 sts | 12 – 17 sts | 11 – 14 sts | 8 – 11 sts | 5 – 9 sts |
| Recommended Hook in Metric Size Range. | Steel 1.6 – 1.4mm | 2.25 – 3.5mm | 3.5 – 4.5mm | 4.5 – 5.5mm | 5.5 – 6.5mm | 6.5 – 9mm | 9mm and larger |
| Recommended Hook US Size Range. | Steel 6, 7, 8 Regular Hook B-1 | B-1 to E-9 | E-4 to 7 | 7 to I-9 | I-9 to K10½ | K10½ to M-13 | M-13 and larger |

# Choices of Yarn

The main choices available are:

*Wool Yarn*

This is an excellent choice for practicing as it's easy to unravel and rework.

*Cotton Yarn*

This is an inelastic fiber which makes it slightly more challenging than wool.

*Acrylic Yarn*

This is very popular yarn as it's available in a variety of colors and it's also affordable.

## The other less common options are:

*Hand Dyed Yarn* – this can add depth and a unique quality to your knitted pieces.

*Variegated Yarn* – this changes color throughout the yarn. The slipped stitches have got an exceptional ability for highlighting various areas of the yarn strands that are variegated.

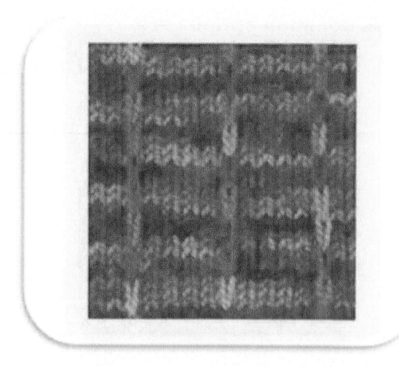

*Mill Dyed Yarn* – predictable and solid. In the slip-stitch patterns, the even saturated commercial tones that are dyed offer a predictable and reliable outcome. Gives a complete control over how and where each color should occur.

*Color Changing Yarn* – A long-striping yarn that repeats usually surrender control over the placement of color and the results will not only delight you but also surprise you. The restrained color shift in these yarns is beautifully highlighted in the slipstitch pattern.

*Watch this* video on how to choose the right yarn for your knitting project

# Needles for Beginners

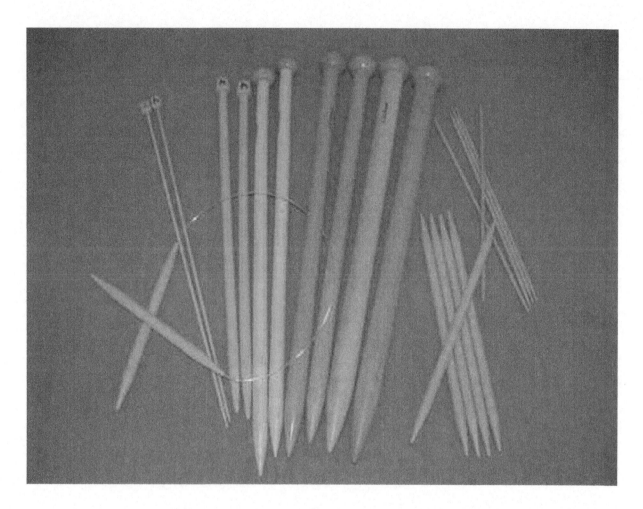

There are several types of needles available on the market and they come in different materials such as *rosewood, aluminum, bamboo* or *casein*. **Patterns will often state the size of needle needed, but the material is more a preference of the user**. As you develop your talent for the craft, you will likely discover which type suits you best.

Many experienced knitters love **wooden or bamboo needles** due to their warmth, the natural feel on their hands and also the comfort and quiet clicking sound that they make. Due to the fact that the needles have quite a bit of friction, they are suitable for slick yarn knitting that can help maintain the stitches, stopping them from sliding away from the needles.

**Metallic needles** are sturdy, heavy and quite hard to break. It is easy to knit very quickly with them as they are slick, but your work can slide off and the loud click can get annoying. Some knitter's report that they are too cold to work with in winter, so may not be the best choice for starting out.

In terms of texture and weight, **plastic needles** are similar to bamboo and wooden needles, which means that you can knit quickly with them. The only disadvantage is that they lack warmth. They may be good to start with as they are very flexible in their abilities.

*Video on* *what are the best knitting needles*

# Needle Types

There are three basic types of knitting needles to consider.

## *The Straight Type*

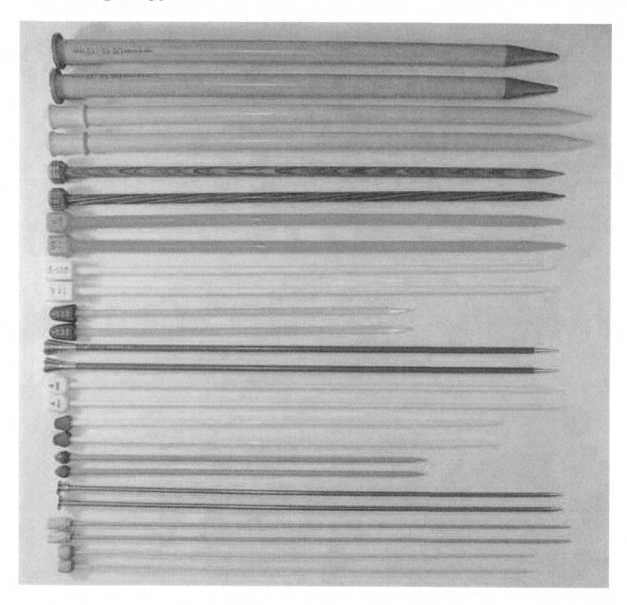

The classic knitting needle is a straight one and contains a single blunt end and a single pointed end. The straight needles vary in length ranging between 9 to 14 inches (22.8 to 35.5 cm) in length.

## *The Circular Type*

The circular knitting needles contain a thin cable that joins together two short needles which can vary in length. As opposed to knitting back and forth, these needles are used for knitting in a circular manner in a seamless round. The length of the needle that you will need, depends on what you're knitting.

## The Double/Pointed Type

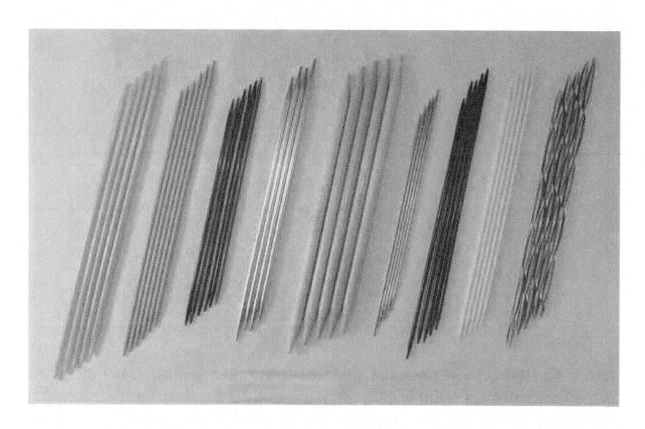

These types of needles have points on each of the ends. They are usually designed for knitting a small round circumference like the sleeves, cuffs and socks.

# Choosing Your Needle

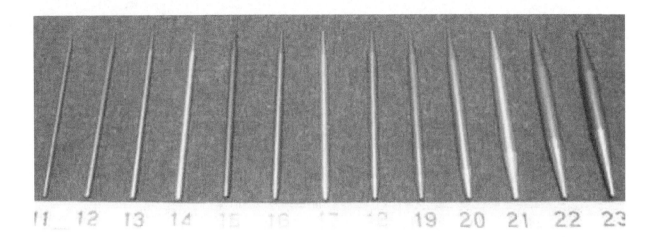

11  12  13  14  15  16  17  18  19  20  21  22  23

Experience shows that it is much simpler to **begin by working with straight needles** as circular patterns are much more challenging to complete. Once you get used to moving the needles from one hand to the other after every row, and you have practiced all of the basic back and forth skills, then it'll be easier to progress.

Beginners are also very fearful of the **double pointed needles**. Nevertheless, it does not take too much time for one to master them and one can be glad that they tried them out. This is especially so when you want to make hats, sleeves, mittens or any other item that is usually knit in the round by just a few stitches.

Note that when you purchase a set of needles that are double pointed; you will in most cases get a package of five needles. For some reason, Americans always tend to use four of them. Stitches are spread across three and then the fourth one is used to knit. On the other hand, Europeans normally space out their stitches across the four needles and use the fifth to knit. It is not unless you have very large socks with many stitches, in most cases the four/needle method is usually the best and you then have only one less needle to deal with.

*Video on* <u>*how to choose the knitting needle*</u>

# Knitting Needle Sizes and Conversions

Size is something else that needs to be taken into consideration. Patterns will often tell you the most suitable needle size, but it's always handy to be aware of the conversion chart:

| METRIC SIZES(mm) | US SIZES | UK/CANADIAN |
|---|---|---|
| 2.0 | 0 | 14 |
| 2.25 | 1 | 13 |
| 2.75 | 2 | 12 |
| 3.0 | - | 11 |
| 3.25 | 3 | 10 |
| 3.5 | 4 | - |
| 3.75 | 5 | 9 |
| 4.0 | 6 | 8 |
| 4.5 | 7 | 7 |
| 5.0 | 8 | 6 |
| 5.5 | 9 | 5 |
| 6.0 | 10 | 4 |
| 6.5 | 10 1/2 | 3 |
| 7.0 | - | 2 |
| 7.5 | - | 1 |
| 8.0 | 11 | 0 |
| 9.0 | 13 | 00 |
| 10.0 | 15 | 000 |
| 12.0 | 17 | - |
| 16.0 | 19 | - |
| 19.0 | 35 | - |
| 25.0 | 50 | - |

*Watch video on choosing a needle size*

# A Journal for Knitting

It's a great idea to **keep a knitting journal for your records**. Noting relevant details down can help you for future reference and assist you on new projects:

- What was the project?

- Where was the pattern from?

- What equipment did you use?

- What needle type and size did you use?

- What materials did you use?

- Where did you buy all of your equipment?

- What problems did you experience?

- What did you learn from the project?

Some photos may also be useful to help you remember past projects. All of this information will become very useful when you want to create your own patterns and techniques for your own projects.

# Other Necessary Tools

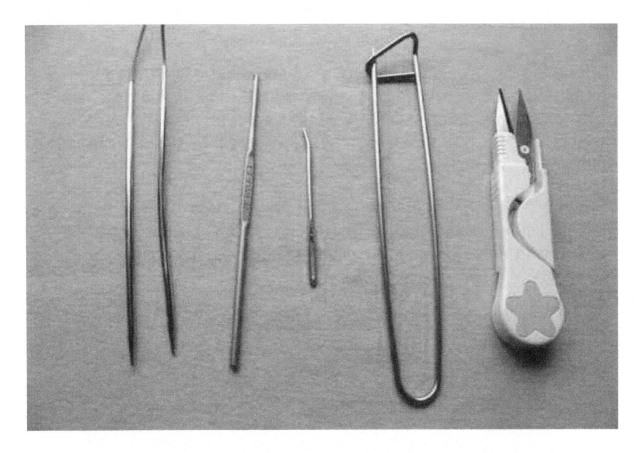

Of course, we know that needles and yarn are utterly essential to a knitting project, but there are other things you must remember, and noting their usage in your journal will help you remember when and where you're likely to need them.

## Scissors

A pair of scissors is necessary for cutting excessive yarn from your project. A pair of school scissors or a special pair of crafting scissors will suffice.

## Sewing Needles

Sewing needles are very beneficial for weaving the ends of the knitting project and also for sewing together the garment's pieces, for example attaching the arms to a sweater. Sewing needles are available in metal or plastic, and which one you choose will depend on your preference.

*Crochet Hooks*

Crocheting is a skill that goes hand-in-hand with knitting and combining the two can have a lovely effect. Even if you don't want to incorporate this other skill, a hook is useful for techniques such as French Hooks. For most yarn weights, size H or G is the most suitable.

With the aforementioned tools, your first knitting project is good to go. The list is not exhaustive but the above basic tools will keep you moving with ease for most of your knitting projects.

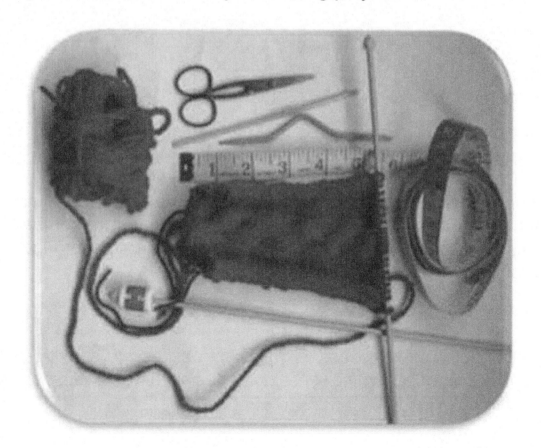

*Watch video on* _essential knitting tools_

# Getting Started with Patterns

Now that you are aware of all of the equipment you need, the next step is to **look into picking a pattern to work from.** You may already know what you want to create, but it's easier to start with something basic as you get to grip with the stitches.

Even patterns aimed at beginners will be written in a very specific way, using coding. As you practice the craft, you'll become very accustomed to it, but to start with it can seem confusing. In this chapter, this code will be explained.

*Watch video on how to work from a knitting pattern.*

# Pattern Basics

## *Skill Level*

This is one of the first things you'll see on a pattern, after the picture and name of the finished piece. This is extremely useful information as you will instantly know if it is achievable for you. Some patterns will write this as a scale of one to four, which is an indication of difficulty, one being the easiest.

## *Size*

If you want to make a fitted piece, such as clothing items, sizing is very important. For beginner patterns, such as scarves and blankets, this won't matter, but it is something to always be aware of for when you become more proficient.

## *Gauge*

The gauge helps you decipher the number of stitches per inch, so before making complex garments, you need to check the gauge to ensure that it will fit. The gauge will tell you how many stitches are needed to make a certain size piece.

It is ***important to remember***:

- The thicker the yarn, the fewer stitches per inch.

- The larger the needle, the bigger the stitches.

- The bigger the stitches, the fewer stitches per inch.

- The thinner the yarn, the more stitches per inch.

- The smaller the needle, the smaller the stitches.

- The smaller the stitches, the more stitches per inch.

*Video on <u>how to make and measure a Gauge Swatch</u>*

## Pattern Information

The pattern information tells you what yarn, needle size and special tools are needed to create the piece. Although you do not have to use the exact yarn suggested in the pattern, it's best to use a yarn of similar thickness and weight.

## Pattern Abbreviations

Most of the patterns are abbreviated heavily to make them quicker to read. However, when you're a beginner they can be challenging to follow. Most importantly, you need to know:

- **CO -** 'Cast On'. This is the number of stitches that you will need to have the project completed.

- **K** - 'Knit'. This is the basic knitting stitch which makes up the majority of most easy projects.

- **P -** 'Purl'. This is the second most common stitch in knitting. It's the opposite of 'Knit' and most of the basic patterns make use of the two, which is often referred to as the Stockinet Stitch.

- **RS** - 'Right Side'. This is the front of the project.

- **WS** - 'Wrong Side'. This is the back of the project.

- **BO -** 'Binding Off'. This is the process of removing the needles from the project.

# Standard Abbreviations for Knitting Patterns

Below you will find all of the **standard abbreviations that are used in knitting**, the various patterns together with their translations.

**alt:** It means alternate (Like the "alt rows")

**beg:** It means begin/beginning

**bet:** It means between

**BO:** It means bind off

**CA:** It means color A (This is the case where there is more than 1 color being used)

**CB:** It means color B (Just as above)

**CC:** It means contrasting color

**cm**: Centimeters

**cn:** It means cable needle

**CO**: It means cast on

**cont.:** It means continue

**dec:** It means decrease/decreases/decreasing

**DK:** It means double knitting (a yarn weight or knitting technique)

**dp, dpn:** It means double-pointed needle

**EON:** It means end of needle

**EOR:** It means end of row

**fL:** It means front loop

**foll:** It means follow or following

**g:** It means gram

**G st:** It means garter stitch (knitting every row)

**inc:** It means increase

**incl:** It means including

**K:** It means knit

**K1 f&b:** It means knit into the front of the stitch and later on to the back of the similar stitch

**k tbl:** It means knitting through the back loop, which establishes a twist on the completed stitch

**k2 tog tbl:** It means knit two stitches together

**k2tog:** It means knit two stitches together through the back loop instead of the front

**kwise:** knitwise

**LC:** It means left cross, a cable stitch where the front of the cross slants to the left

**LH:** It means left hand

**lp(s):** It means loop(s)

**lt:** It means left twist, a stitch that creates a mock cable slanted to the left

**m:** It means meters

**M1:** It means make 1 stitch, which requires an increase method

**M1 p-st**: It means make 1 purl stitch

**MC:** It means main color

**mm**: Millimeters

**oz**: Ounce

**P:** It means purl

**P tbl:** It means purl through the back loop instead of the front

**P up:** It means pick up

**p2tog**: It means purl two stitches together

**P2tog tbl:** It means purl two stitches together through the back loop instead of the front

**pat(s) or patt:** It means pattern(s)

**pm:** It means place stitch marker

**pop**: popcorn bobble

**prev:** It means previous

**psso:** It means mean pass slipped stitch over (as in binding off)

**pu:** It means pick up (stitches)

**pwise**: It means purl-wise

**RC:** It means right cross, a cable stitch where the front of the cross slants to the right

**rem:** It means remain/remaining

**rep:** It means repeat(s)

**rev St st**: It means reverse stockinette stitch

**RH:** It means right hand

**rnd(s):** It means round(s); when knitting on a circular or double pointed needle when it means the yarn is joined, you knit in rounds, not rows

**RS:** It means right side

**RT:** It means right twist, a stitch that creates a mock cable slanted to the right

**sk:** It means skip

**sk2p:** It means slip 1 stitch, knit 2 together, and then pass the slipped stitch over the knitted ones to create a double decrease

**skp:** It means slip 1 stitch, knit 1 stitch, and then pass the slipped stitch over the knitted one to create a single decrease

**sl, slst, slip:** It means slip or slide a stitch without working it

**sl, k1, psso:** It means same as "skp"

**sl1k:** It means slip 1 stitch knit-wise

**sl1p:** It means slip 1 stitch purl-wise

**sl st:** slip stitch(es)

**ss:** slip stitch (in Canadian patterns)

**Ssk:** It means slip 1 stitch, slip the next stitch, and then knit the 2 stitches together to create a left/slanting decrease

**Ssp:** It means slip 1 stitch, slip the next stitch, and then purl the 2 stitches together to create a right/slanting decrease

**Sssk:** It means slip 1 stitch, slip the next stitch, slip the 3rd and then knit the 3 stitches together to create a double, left/slanting decrease

**st:** It means stitch

**sts:** It means stitches

**St st:** It means Stockinette stitch; alternately knit a row and purl a row

**Tbl:** It means through the back loop (of a stitch)

**Tog:** It means together

**WS:** It means wrong side

**wyib:** It means with yarn in back

**wyif:** It means with yarn in front

**Yds:** Yards

**yfwd:** It means yarn forward (same as yarn over)

**Yo:** It means yarn over, move yarn to the opposite direction

**Yrn:** It means yarn 'round' needle (same as yarn over)

**yo**: yarn over

**yon**: It means yarn over needle (yarn over)

**[ ]**: It means work instructions in brackets as many times as directed

**( )**: It means work instructions in parenthesis as directed (also used to indicate size changes)

**\*\***: It means repeat instructions after asterisks as directed

**\***: It means repeat pattern following asterisk as directed.

# How to Read a Pattern

Using the abbreviations, **knitting patterns are written in rows or rounds**. At first this might seem daunting, but once you pull the pieces apart it is very simple.

Example: ***Row 1: \*K2, P2; rep from \* across, end K2.***

Which means that you need to knit the first two stitches, then purl the following two. You'll then repeat this across the row, ending on two knitted stitches.

Sometimes a pattern can also be written in the form of a chart. This is aimed at much more advanced knitters, but for more information on this, please watch *this video*.

# How to Hold the Needles and Yarn

Now that you have selected the pattern you wish to work on, and you have figured out the instructions, you will want to begin. So now you need to know the best ways to hold the needles. Of course, everyone has their own methods, but below is a good starting point.

## The Right Hand Needle

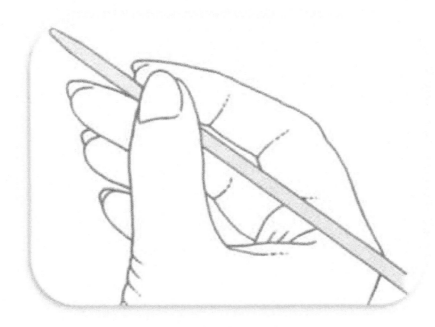

The right hand needle should be held like a pen. When working on the first few rows and casting, the knitted piece should be passed over the hand between the index finger and the thumb. As you progress with the work, your thumb will slide under the piece that is knitted.

## The Left Hand Needle

The left hand needle should be held lightly over the top of the right hand needle, with your thumb and index finger, in order to control the needle's tip.

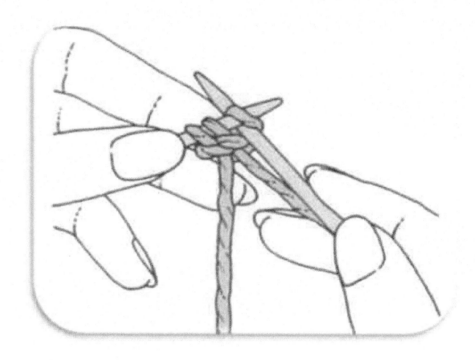

# How to Hold the Yarn

Holding your yarn is also done according to the knitter's preference, but below is a good place to start for beginners.

Using your right hand, weave the yarn through your fingers (as shown in the diagram below). This will allow you to pass the yarn around the top of the needle using your index finger. This allows you to hold the yarn securely and have a lot of control over its tension.

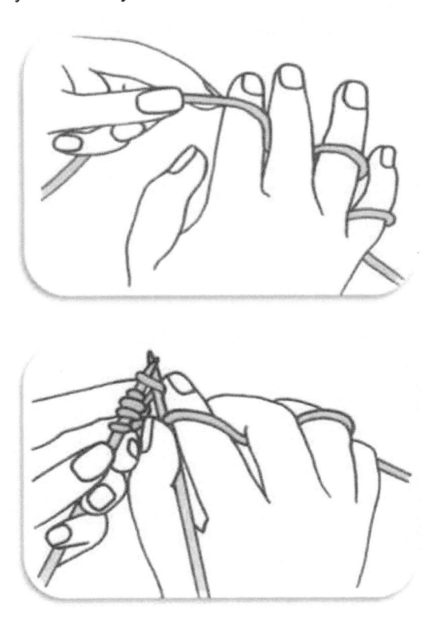

*Video on* <u>*how to hold needles and yarn*</u>

# Stitches

Once you have selected your pattern, you will need to start completing a range of stitches according to the instructions.

This chapter gives you **step-by-step directions for the majority of the stitches** that you'll encounter.

# Casting On Stitches

**Skill Level:** Beginner

**Yarn**: Any

**Needle:** Straight type

**Tools:** Scissors

**All knitting starts with Casting on**. This involves creating loops on the needle which will go on to become the first row of stitches.

*Watch video on <u>Cast On</u>*

There are four **commonly used Cast On techniques**:

*Single Cast On, Longtail Cast On, Knitted Cast On* and *Cable Cast On.*

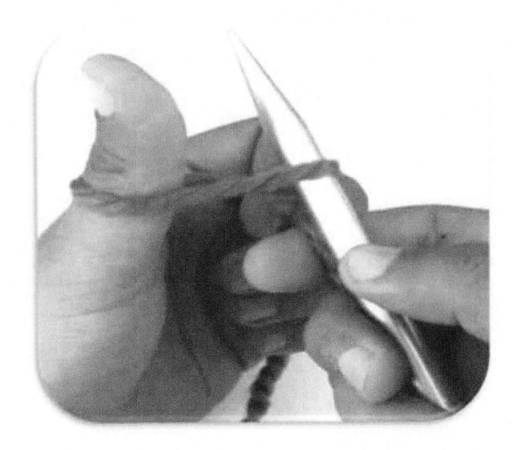

### Single Cast On

1. Make a loop with the yarn

2. Bring the yarn through the loop, creating another loop with a knot at the end.

3. Slide the knot (known as a Slip Knot) onto the needle and pull it tight.

4. Wrap the working yarn around your thumb.

5. Bring the needle under and up through the loop on your thumb.

6. Remove your thumb from the loop and pull the yarn.

7. Repeat steps 4 to 6 until you have the desired number of stitches.


*Watch video on How to do a Single Cast On Method*

## Longtail Cast On

For this method, before you start to cast on, leave a tail at the end of the yarn. The length of the tail depends on the number of stitches you want to cast on. If you want to cast on 10 stitches leave about a foot of yarn for the tail.

1. Drape the tail over your thumb and pointer finger on your left hand.

2. Catch it in between your pointer and middle finger.

3. Catch the yarn connected to the ball against your palm with your pinky and ring fingers.

4. Take the needle in your right hand. Place it on top of the yarn between your thumb and pointer finger.

5. Draw the yarn towards you with the needle. You should see a loop of yarn around your thumb.

6. Bring the needle under the outer piece of yarn next to your thumb and up through the loop.

7. Bring the needle back towards your pointer finger.

8. Bring the needle over the yarn connected to your pointer finger and then under back towards the thumb.

9. Drop the head of the needle back down through the loop around your thumb.

10. Release your thumb from the loop and pull the yarn.

11. Repeat from step 6 until you have the desired number of stitches casted on.

Longtail Cast on with stockinette

Long Tail Cast -on with ribbing

*Watch video on [How to do a Longtail Cast On](#)*

## Knitted Cast On

1. Make a Slip Knot (explained above) and put it on your needle. Hold this needle in your left hand and take the second needle in your right hand.

2. Pass the needle in the right hand through the loop on the left needle and bring the right needle under the left needle.

3. With your left hand, wrap the working yarn around your left hand needle.

4. Bring the right needle back through the loop on the left needle.

5. Now you have a loop around your right needle. Turn the loop and drop it on to the left needle and release the right needle from the loop.

6. Pull the yarn and you have two stitches casted on.

7. To continue, repeat from step 2.

*Watch video on Knitted Cast On*

## Cable Cast On

1. For the first two stitches, use instructions for knitted cast on.

2. Once you have two stitches casted on. Take your right needle and put it in between the two stitches by bringing it under the left needle and through the yarn that connects the two stitches.

3. Wrap the working yarn around the right needle.

4. Bring the right needle back through the loops.

5. Now you have a loop around your right needle. Turn the loop and drop it on to the left needle and release the right needle from the loop.

6. Pull the yarn. You should have two stitches casted on.

7. To continue, repeat from step 2.


*Watch video on Cable Cast On*

# The Basic Bind-Off

**Skill Level:** Beginner

**Yarn:** Any

**Needle:** Straight Type

**Tools:** Scissors

Binding off is the process where the stitches are removed from the needles and secured to keep the piece intact. This is an easy process to master, which can be adapted to work on either side of your work.

1. Knit two stitches. Insert the top of the left needle into the first stitch on the right needle. Lift the stitch over the last stitch you knit and over the top of the right needle.

2. One stitch remains on the right needle. Knit another stitch. Lift that stitch over the stitch just knit.

**3.** Continue in this way until one loop remains. Cut the yarn, leaving a tail of 4 or 5 inches and draw the end through the last stitch.

*Watch video on the knitting Bind Off*

# The Knit Stitch

**Skill Level:** Beginner

**Yarn:** Any

**Needle:** Straight Type

**Tools:** N/A

## Step 1 - The Beginning

The Knit Stitch is the basis of all knitting. Once you have learnt how to cast on and bind off, the knit stitch is all you need for very basic patterns such as washcloths and afghans.

Once you have cast on the appropriate number of stitches according to the pattern, you can begin with the knit stitch.

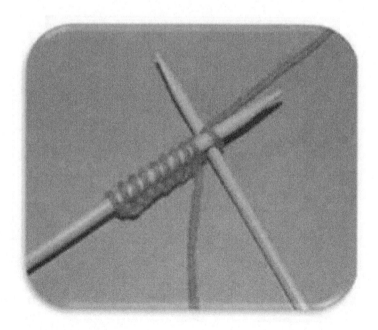

Opening the loop is the first step used to form the knit stitch. Hold the empty needle in your right hand and the needle with the stitches in your left hand. The working yarn should then be to the back of the work. The stitches should face you and the bumpy loops part facing towards your body. Ensure to work through the single loop as opposed to the bumpy part when forming your stitches. Insert point of right needle in first stitch, from front to back, just as in casting on

The three photos show how the knit stitch is made in what is referred to as the *English*. It can also be called the *American, right handed or throwing style* where the yarn is usually held by the right hand. *Continental style* is yet another option, it is also referred as the *picking or German* whereby the yarn is held on the left hand side.

## Step 2 – Wrap the Yarn

With right index finger, bring yarn from ball under and over point of right needle:

Upon getting the needle in place, carry the working yarn simply and hold it with your right hand and at the same time over the needle on the right hand. You should then go counter clockwise all round the needle and ensure that the working yarn is sliding between both needles. This is the yarn that makes the loop new and that which enables your knitting to be a complete project.

## Step 3 – Turn the Stitch

Draw yarn through stitch with right needle point:

Slide the right hand needle to the front of the left-handed needle starting from the back. Ensure to keep the yarn's loop on the left hand side of the needle for the moment but punch through together with the working yarn so that it is able to make a loop on the needle's right hand. For you to do this, the right hand needle should be left to slide down in order for the loop to get closer to the needle's tip and ensure it does not slide off. When the needle's tip gets close to the edge of the needle's left handle, exert a little push to the right hand needle in order for it to move in front of the needle's left hand.

## Step 4 – Finishing the Stitch

This step now differs from casting on: Slip loop on left needle off, so new stitch is entirely on right needle.

This completes one knit stitch. Repeat Steps 1 through 4 in each stitch still on left needle. When the last stitch is worked, one row of knitting is completed.

## Step 5 – How to Proceed

When all the stitches have moved from the left hand needle, a process known as 'turning the work' begins. You only require flipping over the work. Temporarily, the front side now becomes the back. This needle should be moved from your right hand and back to the left hand side and you will discover that you will be right back where you begun. All the above steps should now be repeated for you to continue knitting this row, the next and the net. You will realize that you are now knitting.

*Watch video on Knit stitch.*

# The Purl Stitch

**Skill Level:** Beginner

**Yarn:** Any

**Needle:** Straight Type

**Tools:** N/A

Put simply, ***purling is backwards knitting***. Knitted stitches appear lower and flat, and the purl stitches are higher and bumpier. Together they create an advanced looking knitted piece.

The steps for purling are as shown below.

## Step 1

Just like it is done in the knit stitch, the working needle should be held in the right hand and the needle containing the stitches should be in your left hand. The yarn is then held and also manipulated with the right hand and kept to the work's front.

The right needle should be inserted from the back towards the front to the first stitch on the needle in the left hand side. The needle on the right should be in front of the left needle and similarly, the yarn should be at the front of the work.

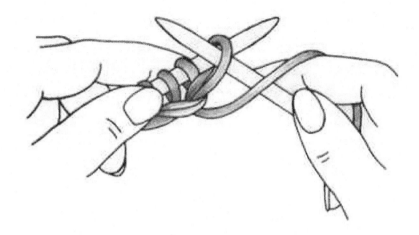

## Step 2

Bring the yarn in your right hand toward the tip of the right needle. Using the right index finger, the yarn should be wrapped clockwise around the needle on the right. Be careful not to wrap it around the left needle.

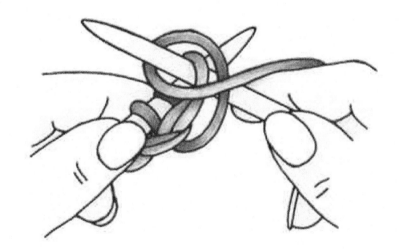

## Step 3

The right needle and yarn should be drawn backwards through the stitch on and the left needle thereby forming on the right needle, a loop.

The stitch should then be slipped off the needle on the left. One purl stitch will have been made. These steps should then be repeated in the subsequent stitches till all the stitches have been worked from the needle in the left. You will have made a row of these purl stitches.

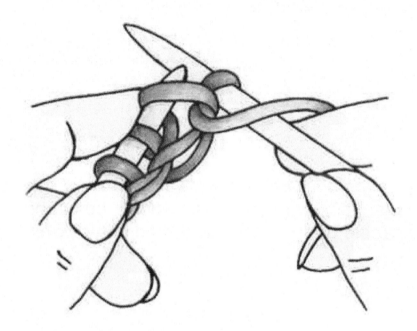

*Watch video on the Purl Stitch*

# The Garter Stitch

**Skill Level:** Beginner

**Yarn:** Any

**Needle:** Straight Type

**Tools:** N/A

In simple terms, the **Garter Stitch is a row of knitted or purled stitches**. It's easily identified by the horizontal ridges formed by the tops of the knitted loops on every other row. The

Garter stitch produces a really beautiful effect which can work for edges and borders, as well as garments.

**Step 1 -** To knit a garter stitch, you need to start by holding the yarn in your right hand, and holding the needle containing the cast on stitches in your left.

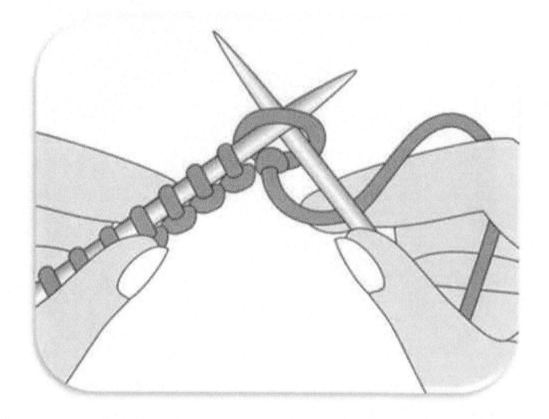

**Step 2** - Insert the tip of the right hand needle into the first stitch on the left hand needle, from left to right and front to back.

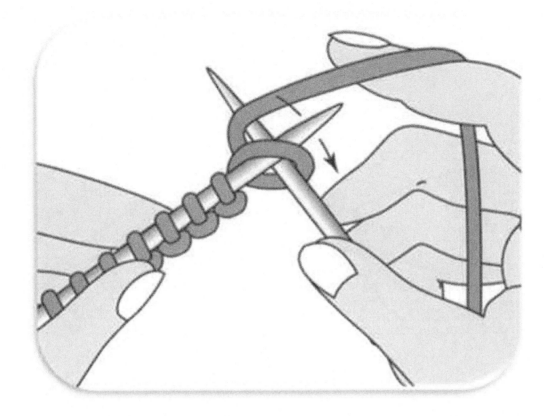

**Step 3** - With your right hand, bring the yarn to the front from the left side of the right hand needle, over the needle and down through the middle of the needles.

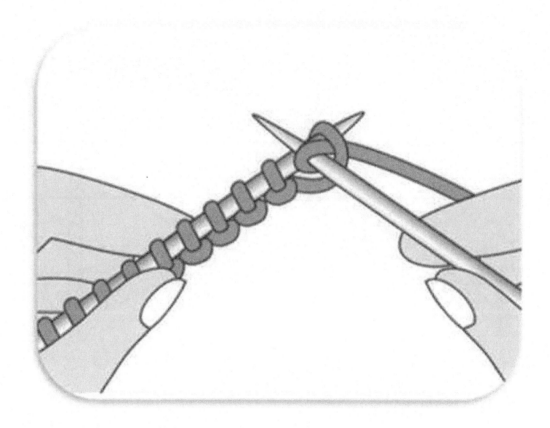

**Step 4** - Keep slight tension on the wrapped yarn and bring the tip of the needle in your right hand – with the yarn – through the loop on the needle in your left hand.

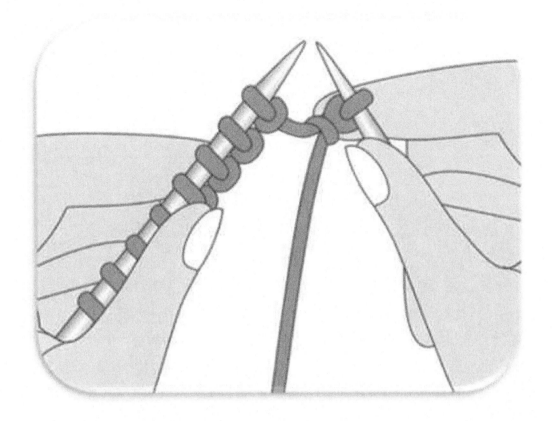

**Step 5** - Slide the needle in your right hand to the right, until the loop on the left hand needle drops off.

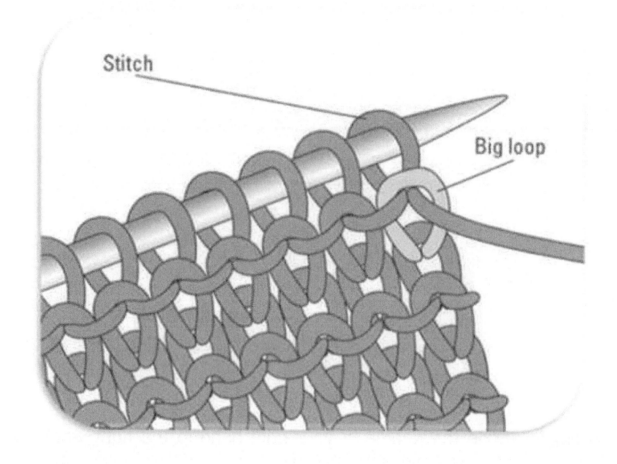

**Step 6** - Repeat the above steps until you've knitted all the stitches from your left hand needle, leaving it empty.

**Step 7** - The right hand needle will now be full, so you need to turn your work and start again.

*Watch video on _Garter Stitch_.*

# The Stockinette Stitch

**Skill Level:** Beginner

**Yarn:** Any

**Needle:** Straight Type

**Tools:** N/A

The Stockinette Stitch is made up of knit and purl stitches. This stitch has a much smoother appearance than the Garter stitch but has the tendency to curl, so it's better suited to rolled cuff and rolled edged scarves.

When creating the Stockinette Stitch, it is important to remember that there is a 'right side' and a 'wrong side'. On the 'right side' the stitch will have the appearance of 'v' shapes.

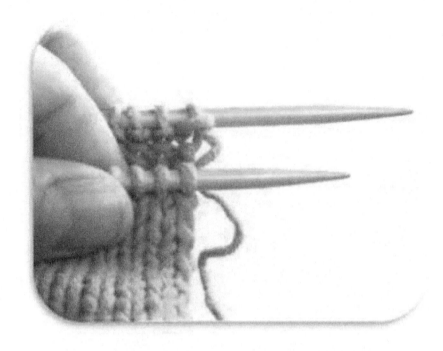

**Step 1 -** Cast on and knit all of the stitches in the first row.

**Step 2** - Swap the needles so that the needle with the stitches is back in your left hand.

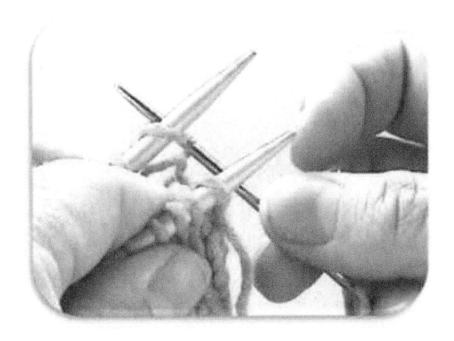

**Step 3** - Purl the next row of stitches.

**Step 4** - Swap the needles again and knit the next row.

**Step 5** - Continue to alternate until you have completed the appropriate number of stitches.

**Step 6** - Once you have finished, then bind off to finish the project.

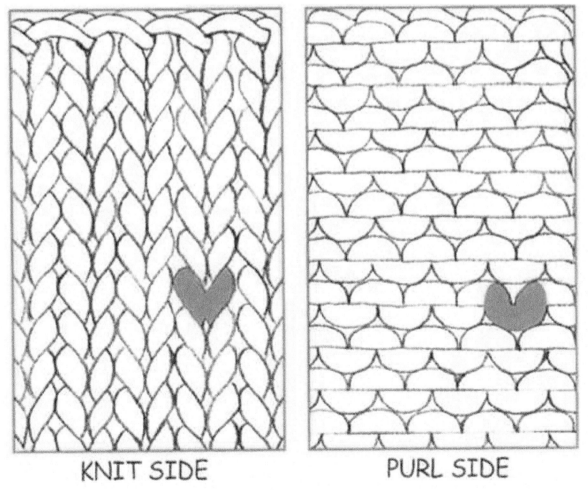

KNIT SIDE           PURL SIDE

*Watch video on <u>Stockinette Stitch</u>*

# Basic Ribbing

**Skill Level:** Beginner

**Yarn:** Any

**Needle:** Straight Type

**Tools:** N/A

The **Rib stitch creates textured vertical stripes**. To knit the Rib stitch, you alternate from knitted to purl stitches within a row (as opposed to alternate rows with the Stockinette stitch). It creates a stretchy material which works well for making necklines, cuffs and hems.

*Single Ribbing*

To create 1x1 ribbing, alternate single knit stitches with single purl stitches. This creates very narrow columns.

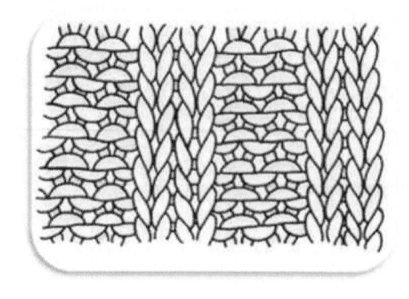

*Double Ribbing*

To create 2x2 ribbing, alternate two knit stitches with two purl stitches. This pulls less than the 1x1 ribbing and produces wider columns.

*Video on Ribbing.*

## How to Move Yarn Back and Forward

When a stitch is knit, the yarn will at all times be held at the back of the work. While making a purl, the yarn rests at the frontend. When changing from to the purl from a knit, you need to ensure that the yarn is at rightful position in order to work the succeeding stitch. When moving yarn to front from back, or the other way round, ensure that the yarn passes over two of the needles.

## Knitwise

## Purlwise

- Now knit one and purl one ribbing (K1, P1)

- Then cast stitches (odd numbers).

- In the right side of the first row, Knit 1 and Purl 1 repeating to the end.

- In the second row, purl 1, knit 1 and repeat to the end. Repeat that in rows 1-2.

- Now knit two and purl two ribbing (K2, P2)

- On a multiple of four stitches and two extra, cast on. Knit 2 and purl 2 on the right side of Row 1 and repeat to the very end. In Row # 2, Purl 2 and knit 2 and repeat to the very end. Rows 1-2 should be repeated.

# Seed Stitch

**Skill Level:** Beginner

**Yarn:** Any

**Needle:** Straight Type

**Tools:** N/A

It is textured in working a series of knit n' purl stitches that alternate on each row. As opposed to ribbing, you will require to purl the knit stitches and knit the purl stitches.

**You will require to Cast on an even number of stitches.**

From the right side of **Row 1**, you will require to Knit 1 and purl 1 and repeat from the beginning to the end.

In **Row 2**, Purl 1 and knit 1 and repeat to the very end.

Rows 1 and 2 should then be repeated again. This is a ribbing, which is broken up on each row.

See, all the bumps resemble seeds. It is a beautiful pattern that is clean looking and the bumps usually add a nice feel and texture. By knitting the purls and purling the knits, it simply means that a knit stitch is put over a purl stitch and vice versa thereby making seeds. It is easy to learn it.

**Bind off** to complete the stitch.

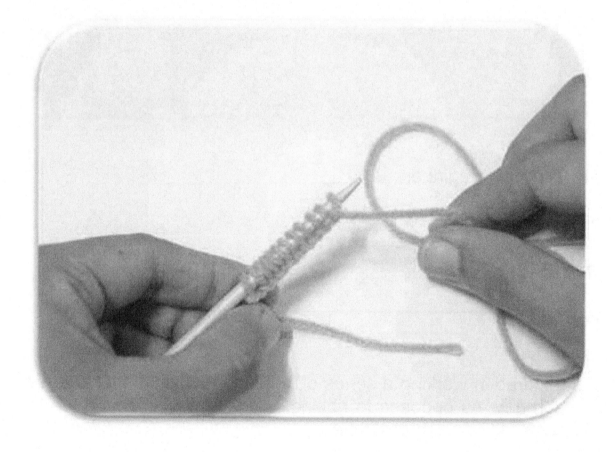

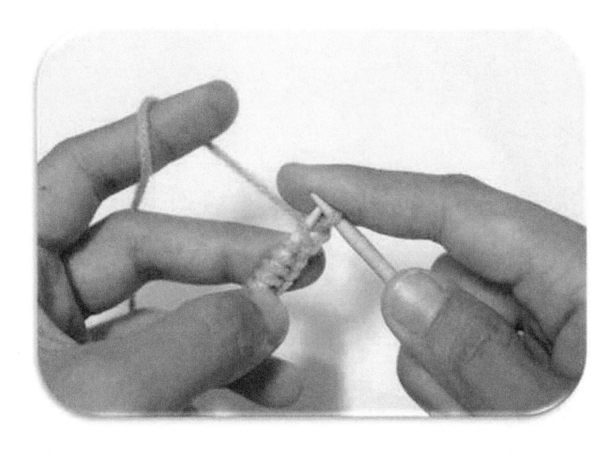

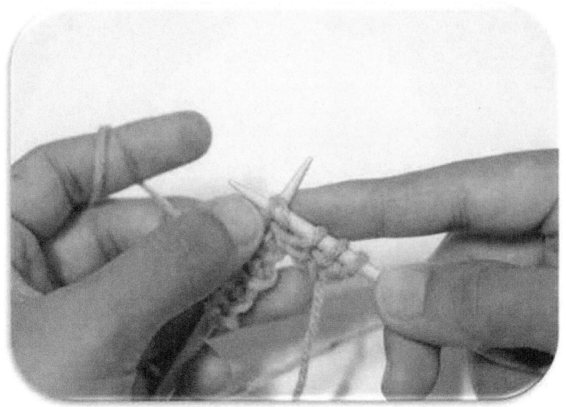

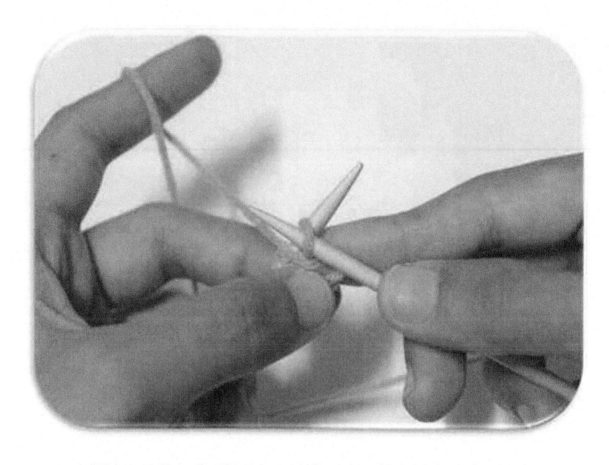

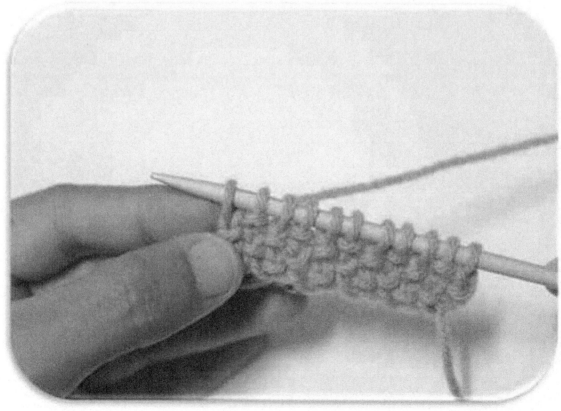

*Video on how to knit Seed Stitch.*

# Double Seed Stitch

**Skill Level:** Beginner

**Yarn:** Any

**Needle:** Straight Type

**Tools:** N/A

An even number of stitches should be cast on.

In the right hand side of **Row 1**, Knit 1 and Purl 1 to the very end.

Repeat Row # 1 in **Row 2**.

In **Row 3**, purl 1 and Knit 1 and repeat to the very end.

Repeat Row # 3 in **Row 4**.

Make a repetition from rows 1 through to the 4th. Repeat from row 1 to 4 till the length you desire.

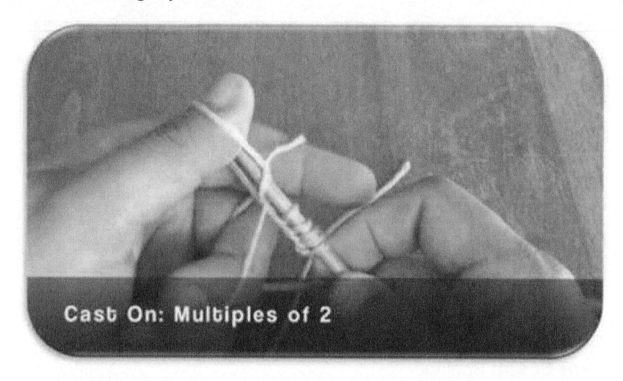

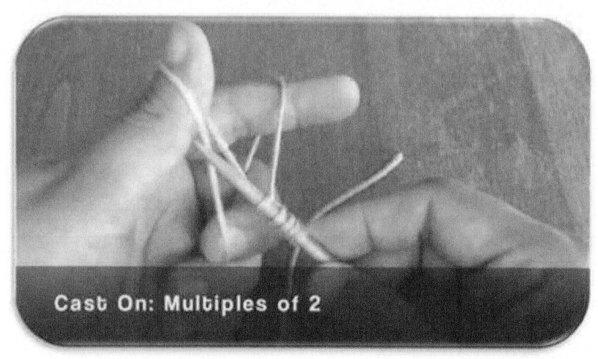

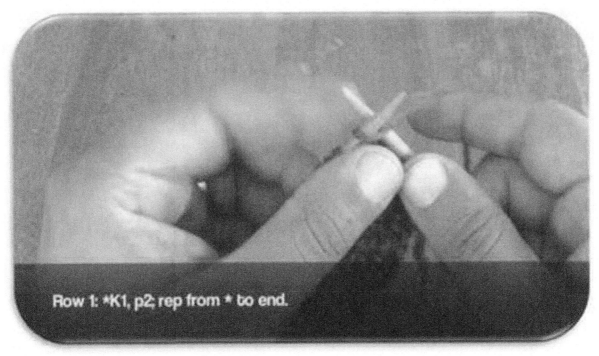

Row 1: *K1, p2; rep from * to end.

Row 1: *K1, p2 rep from * to end.

Row 2: Rep row 1

Row 3: *P1, k1; rep from * to end.

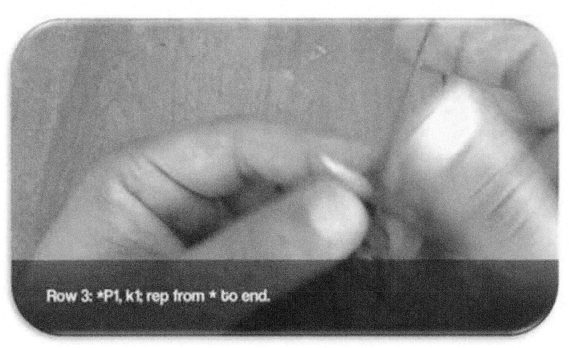

Row 3: *P1, k1; rep from * to end.

Row 4: Rep row 3

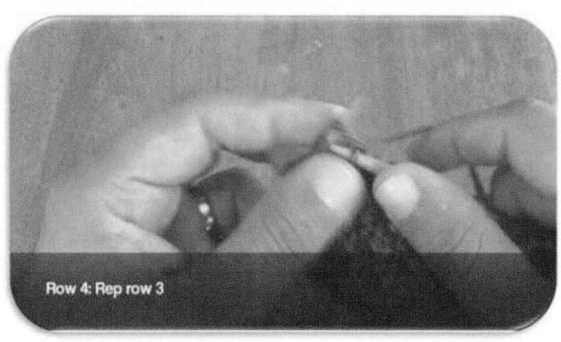

Row 4: Rep row 3

*Watch video on Double Seed Stitch.*

# Roman Stitch

ROMAN STITCH

**Skill Level:** Beginner

**Yarn:** Any

**Needle:** Straight Type

**Tools:** N/A

**The Roman Stitch works on a number of stitches that are all even.**

You require to knit in **Row 1** and Purl in **Row 2**.

Knit 1, Purl 1 in **Row 3** and repeat the whole process across.

In **Row 4**, Purl 1, Knit 1 and repeat from across.

For the pattern, all the four rows need to be repeated. Alternatively, you can knit Rows 1 and 3, purl rows 2 and 4 and also knit the knit and purl rows that are alternating like 5 and 6. Note that both of them will be very much attractive.

Usually, this stitch is commonly found in Eastern embroideries that make a solid band or otherwise used for leaf filing or even other forms that form a mid-rib. Slanted or horizontal stitches can be used for working the stitch.

## How to Work the Roman Stitch

As a working guide, three lines are required. The stitch will then be taken from one side to the nest of the form starting at the left top hand side or tip incase it's a leaf. The needle is inserted in the right hand side in the opposite direction of where the thread came on the left hand side through the fabric. This requires to be left very loose in order to be brought down towards the rib. The needle should then be brought out on the line's center with the point well above the thread as laid across in the below figure.

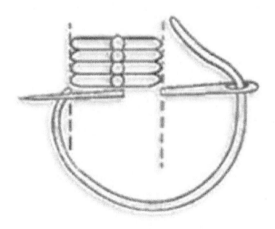

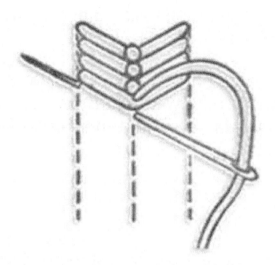

Just below the thread, insert the needle once more while trying it down with just a small notch. The needle is then brought through to the left side again for the proceeding stitch as shown in the diagram below. In case the stitches are left to be slanting like in the below figure, the needle will have to be inserted in a diagonal manner.

The Roman stitch is mostly used in work that is conventional.

*Watch video on <u>how to knit Roman stitch</u>.*

# The Linen Stitch

**Skill Level:** Beginner

**Yarn:** Any

**Needle:** Straight Type

**Tools:** N/A

The Linen Stitch (sometimes referred to as the *Fabric Stitch*) can be made to look totally different – just by changing the color of the yarn used. The fabric created by this stitch is firm and doesn't curl.

## Solid Color Linen Stitch

To create a solid color linen stitch, you need to work with an even number of stitches.

For the **first row**, you'll want to alternate between knitting a stitch, then slipping one with the yarn in the front until you have finished the row.

For the **second row**, you'll want to alternate between purling a stitch, then slipping one with the yarn in the back until you have finished the row.

Repeat these two rows until the piece is complete.


## Two Color Linen Stitch

In order to achieve the two-color pattern as shown, color A should be worked on two rows and color B similarly to two rows.

Once you are through with every two rows, you need to continue alternating colors in every two rows.

The woven effect will be enhanced by the two-color pattern. In order to achieve the best results, Cast with color A and go right to Row 2 before going to use color B in the next two rows.


## Three Color Linen Stitch

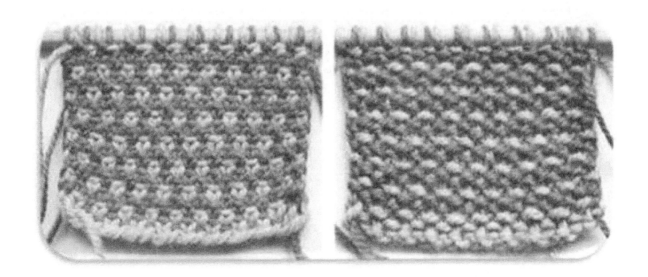

In order to come up with a speckled cool fabric, you may add a third color if you like. By starting with color A, Row 1 will thus be worked and for Row 2, switch to color B and when you go back to Row 1, now use color C. At the end of Row 6, repeat and you will see that every row shall be worked in each color, even if it is not one after the other. Using color A, cast on and proceed to Row 2 using color B.

- Row 1: Color A

- Row 2: Color B

- Row 1: Color C

- Row 2: Color A

- Row 1: Color B

- Row 2: Color C

*Video on* *how to knit linen stitch*.

# Cable and Twist Stitches

**Skill Level:** Intermediate

**Yarn:** Any

**Needle:** Straight Type

**Tools:** N/A

**This type of pattern takes the combination of two or more stitches**. Resultantly, the canvas slopes to the right or left sides. This makes knitting to intertwine the braid. The patterns are therefore referred to as *bundles* or *braids*.

The moving loops are usually done using an additional needle cable. The motion is slightly tilted to the left and one more needle loop leave on the knitting's front side or else with an inclination to the back or right. Most commonly, the sorts of braids are made with decorations of coat and pullovers, warm jerseys, wide scarves, jackets and sweaters.

**Step 1**: Ignore the first stitch on the left-hand needle for a moment and put the right-hand needle into the back of the second stitch on the needle.

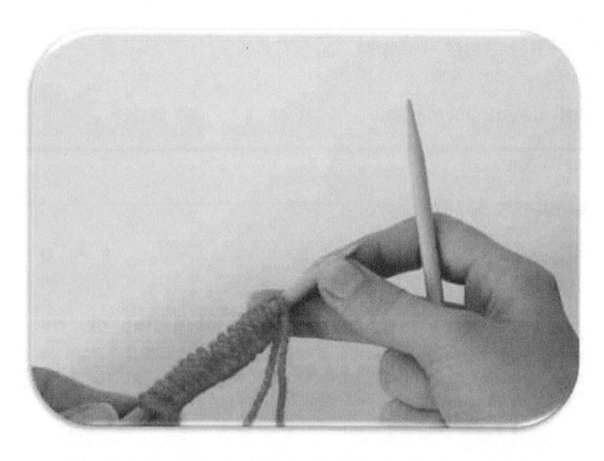

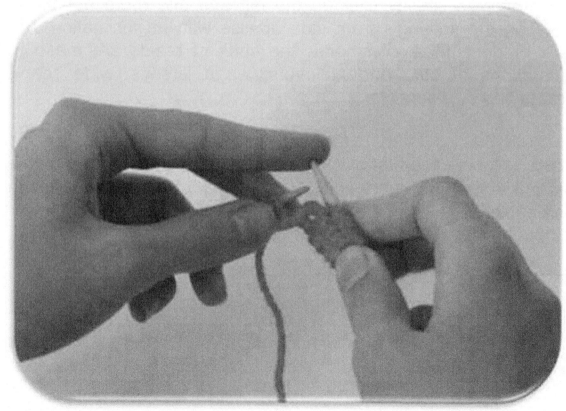

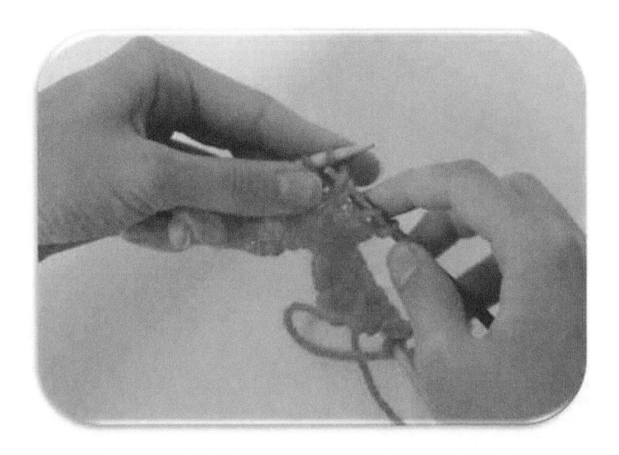

Knit this stitch through the back loop, but don't drop it off the left-hand needle.

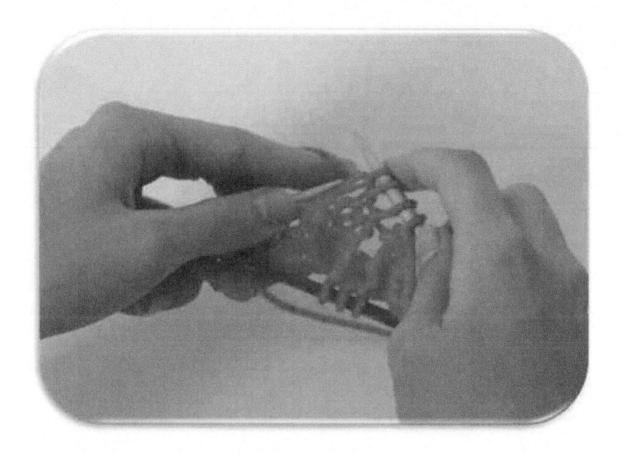

**Step 2**: Bring the needle back around to the front and knit the first stitch normally through the front loop.

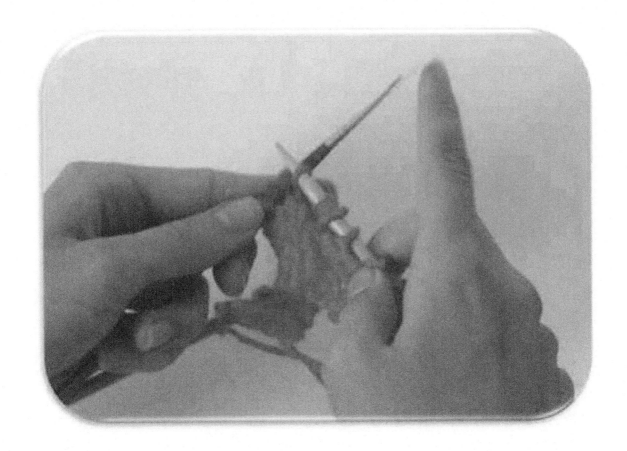

**Step 3**: Drop both stitches from the left-hand needle.

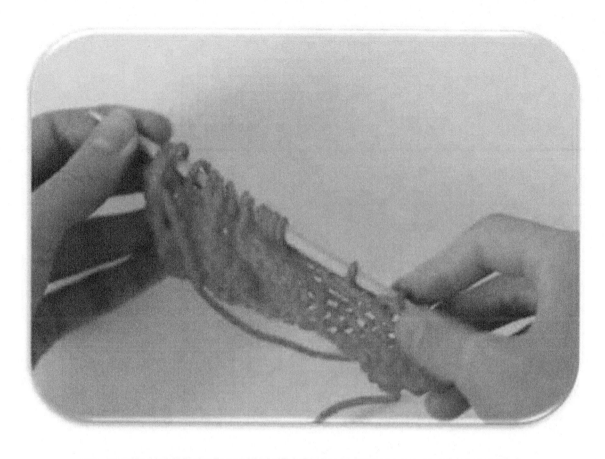

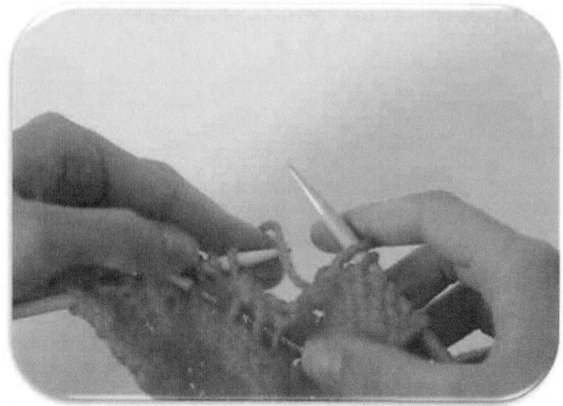

**Step 4**: Repeat Steps 1–3 each time you need to work a twist.

*Below are some examples.*

## Challah

## Dome

**V-Twisted Knit stitch**

**Fence**

*Video on <u>how to knit Cable Stitch</u>.*

*Video on <u>how to knit Twist Stitch</u>.*

# The Bobble Stitch

**Skill Level:** Intermediate

**Yarn:** Any

**Needle:** Straight Type

**Tools:** N/A

As well as being a fun filled word, bobble is a cool technique that is used in adding a three-dimension texture to any knitting project. Bobbles can be added to almost all items. This type of technique is more of an actual stitch and less of a stitch pattern. This means that you will have to do the whole of the bobble procedure at some specific point in your project in knitting.

# How to Knit a Large Bobble

The next few steps have to be completed in order to knit a large bobble:

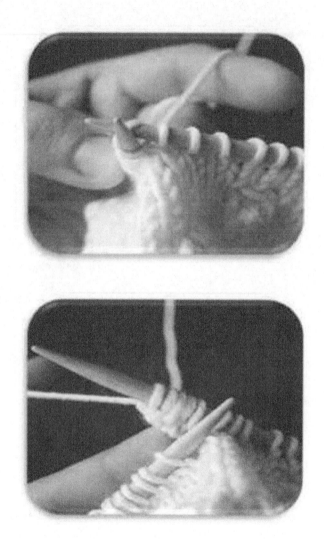

## Step 1

You need to have the stitches increased from 1 to 5. In order to do this, you require knitting to the back and front of the stitch two times without having to pull it off in the left hand side. Knit to the front side again and from the left needle, drop the stitch.

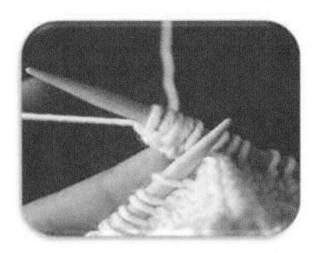

## Step 2

You then need to have your work turned, across the five stitches, purl across before turning once more, now knit across 5, make a turn, across five, purl, turn once again and for the last time, knit across the five as shown.

## Step 3

Decrease downwards to one stitch now. In order for this to be done, the second stitch should be slipped towards the needle on the right four times over the very first stitch. The photo above shows how a completed bobble should look like. The bobble is just an increase into a single stitch and only about four small rows before a decrease back to one. In order to make the bobbles, the tiny rows usually fold onto one another.

## Knitting a Smaller Bobble

Even little bobbles can be knit. They usually have got a delicate texture of 3 dimension small stitches.

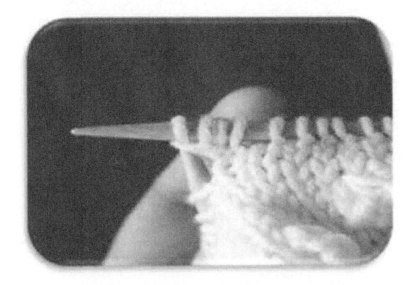

Once you get to the point where you wish to have your bobble placed, the stitches will now be increased to 4 by having to knit to the front part and twice at the back of it.

Across all the four stitches, you need to turn and purl.

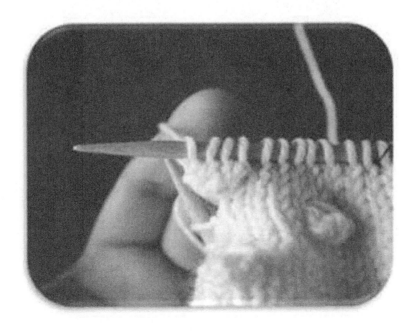

After that, you need to turn and knit across all of them.

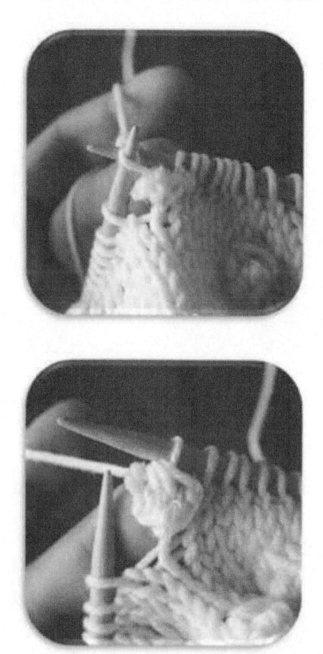

On the right hand side of the needle, you require to slip the second stitch over the first for a number of three times in order to get all the way down to one.

The above photo compares the big bobbles to the little ones. The bobble patterns are especially made for the winter season. Most of the patterns will clearly point to the sort of bobble that should be used.

The above beautiful hats have featured small bobbles fitted in the diagonal pattern. Towards the top, a swirl is created. The hats are specially made for mother and baby.

The bag above has been designed to show how bobbles can create a very fine and beautiful texture.

The bag below is an example of a shoulder bag pattern.

The above bag shows the cowl features all over the bobble pattern features. They are especially suitable for the winter season.

The hat shows a combination of cables and bobbles. See how the bobbles come between some cables and at the side of all others. Together, the cables POP are done.

The scarf around the little girl's neck makes use of bobbles at the edge. This is just an amazing beautiful finishing. These patterns not only add interesting texture but also a cinch on the knit as well.

*Video on how to crochet bobble stitch*.

# Techniques

There are many knitting techniques that help you even further with knitting patterns. A selection of these is discussed in the chapter below.

# Eyelets and Lace Stitches

**Skill Level:** Intermediate

**Yarn:** Any

**Needle:** Straight Type

**Tools:** Crochet Hook

Eyelets are a very pretty looking technique that can add all sorts of interesting designs to your knitting patterns. **An eyelet is a small**

**hole in the fabric the knit fabric**. This is accomplished with a yarn over and a decrease.

First, to make this chain, make five repeats by chaining 15 stitches for three repeats.

Now draw the last chain up over the needle.

Now crochet back to the chain by drawing up one loop in all stitches and pull these up over the needle.

Repeat this until drawn up loop over all stitches in the chain; now transfer them to the needle. This step will create large loops in the lace knitting.

Now slide the hook from the first set of loops and then pull them off the knitting needle.

Now, yarn over, pull from the set of loops on the hook. Work a single crochet for each loop of the set. Continue this till all the loops crocheted. This process will complete the first row of lace!

Now draw loops up from all crochet stitches you made, and repeat steps 1 to 5 till the desired length.

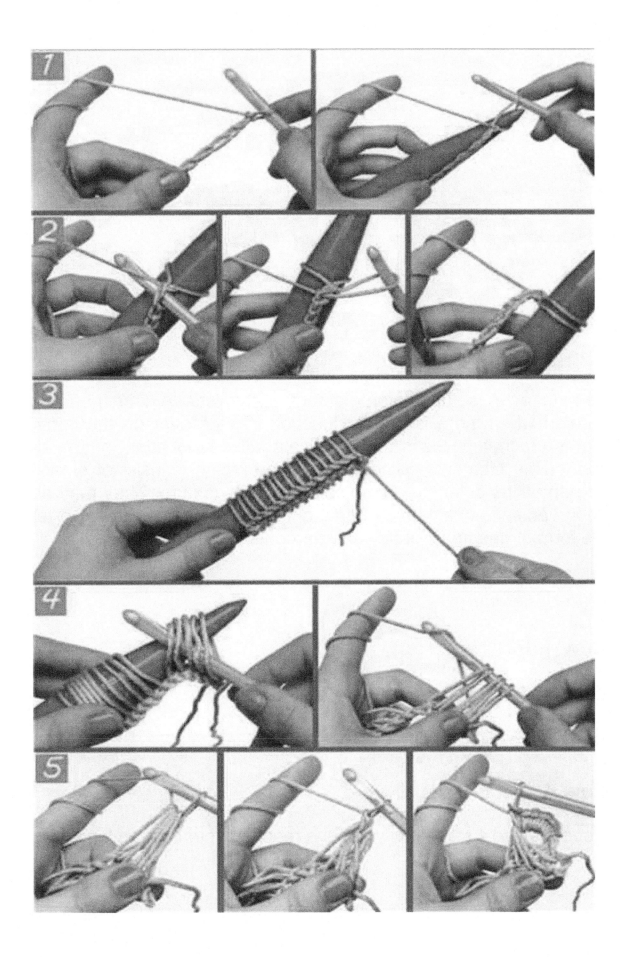

Yarning over is the major element of eyelets. A lace pattern is created when there is regular location of yarn over on the canvas that is crocheted. Sizes of the eyelets differ in location, nature and size of the elements composition. They mainly consist of small or large motives differing in complex or simple texture. They may also be in vertical, horizontal or diagonal in direction, they may also take the form of geometric or flower ornaments.

## Pattern details:

**Row 1** (RS): Knit

**Row 2**: Purl

**Row 3**: K2, * yo, k2 tog, k1; rep from * to end

**Row 4**: Purl

Repeat these 4 rows until you have reached your desired length.

For the openwork products, it is quite important to pick on the right kind of yarn. The yarn needs to be smooth, good quality and of dark in color. The pattern may also look effectively and seen very well. Even then, the yarn's thickness can be quite different ranging from thin summer and elegant too thick for sweaters, pullovers and sports jackets.

Some of the examples include:

**Wings**

**Cookies**

**Dragon fly**

**Peacock tail**

*Video on how to knit the Eyelet Stitch.*

# Zigzag Stitch

**Skill Level:** Intermediate

**Yarn:** Any

**Needle:** Straight Type

**Tools:** N/A

Among the easiest ways of **finishing edges of the seam allowance in a project** is the Zigzag Stitch. The threads around the fabric's edge can be wrapped thus have them locked so that they cannot fray. It is an effective and efficient stitch. There is also the *3 zigzag stitch* or the *multi-step zigzag*. A regular zigzag is usually one stitch from one point to another whereas a 3-step zigzag is done by 3 stitches from point A to point B. Occasionally, on the thinner fabrics, a normal zigzag can have the fabric bunch up. However, a three step zigzag stitch is much flatter as it is just like a straight line from one point to another and prevents the fabric from bunching up.

The Zig Zag Stitch adds a chevron pattern to your knitting. It's great for adding an interesting edging on a garment – such as a scarf.

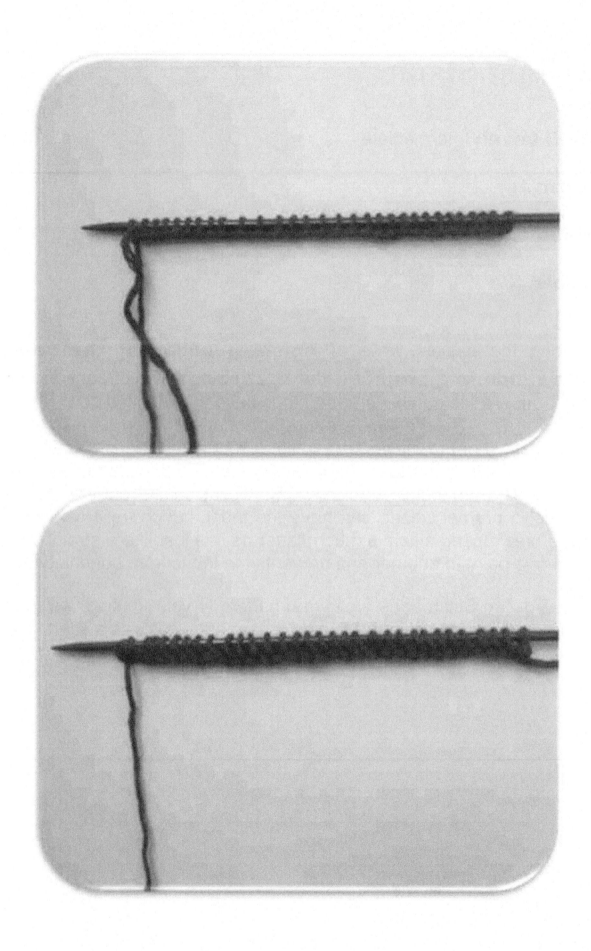

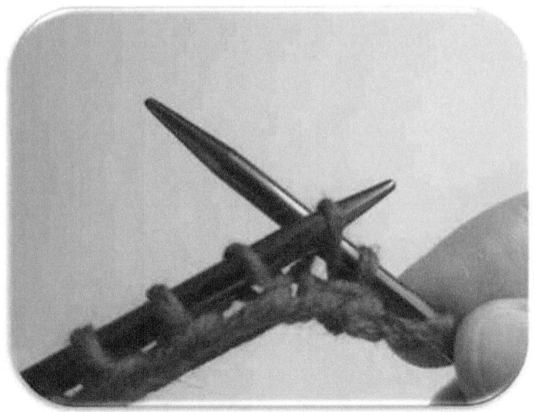

**Pattern Details:**

Cast on a multiple of 14 + 2

**Row 1** and all **odd rows**: Purl

**Row 2** and all **even rows**: K1, knit into the front and back of the next stitch, K4, SSK, K2tog, K4 *Knit into the front and back of the next 2 stitches, K4, SSK, K2tog, K4* Repeat from * to last 2 stitches. Knit into the front and back of the next stitch, K1.

The regular zigzag and the 3-step zigzag stitches may be used for finishing the fabric's raw edges individually. As above, the regular zigzag is done by stitching on the allowance of the seam up to the stitching. The stitching can then be done at any place on the seam allowance that you desire.

*Video on <u>how to make a Zigzag Stitch</u>.*

# Slipping Stitch

**Skill Level:** Intermediate

**Yarn:** Any

**Needle:** Straight Type

**Tools:** N/A

**Slipping a stitch means passing a stitch from one needle to yet another without necessarily working it**. At times, it is done when working the stitch and color pattern as well as when decreasing. That stitch which is slipped purlwise stays untwisted but if it is slipped knitwise, it will twist. If instructions fail to specify the way to have the stitch slipped, you require slipping it purlwise save it for when it is decreasing. At this juncture, the knit stitches should be slipped knitwise while the purl stitches should be slipped knitwise.

In order to **slip a stitch knitwise**, the right needle is inserted into the next stitch in the needle on the left just like the stitch was being knit. The stitch is pulled off the needle in the left. The stitch will be on the needle on the right and is twisted.

**Slipping Stitches Purlwise**: Insert the right needle (from back to front) into the next stitch on the left needle and place it on the right needle without working it.

For any knitter who is new to color knitting, prospects of handling two strands or more of yarn at any one time may seem overwhelming. Apply the slipped stitches magic. You require using only one strand at any time in order to create beautifully looking patterns.

*Video on how to knit slipping stitches.*

*Video on Slip Stitch purlwise.*

*Watch video on Slip Stitch Knitwise.*

# Drop Stitch

**Skill Level:** Intermediate

**Yarn:** Any

**Needle:** Straight Type

**Tools:** N/A

To create a dropped stitch, make a normal knit and purl stitch and ensure that you wrap the yarn all-round the needle two or three times instead of once. This must be repeated on every stitch across the row.

On the next row, knit or purl the stitch and have the extra yarn wraps slide off the needle. At the end of this row, tug the yarn gently to straighten the dropped stitch. The dropped stitch will look like a long knitted stitch.

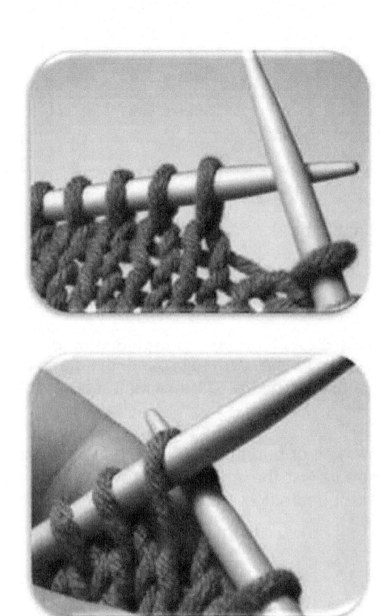

## Pattern Details:

**Row 1**: Knit.

**Row 2**: Knit each stitch, wrapping the yarn around the needle twice instead of once when completing the stitch.

**Row 3**: Knit each stitch, dropping the extra wrap off the needle as you complete each stitch.

*Repeat these three rows for pattern.*

## Using Dropped Stitches

To many projects, dropped stitches are a good addition to most projects on such items as scarves, headbands, scarves and tank tops. Those patterns that make use of the dropped stitch will in general have you knit several plain rows on each side of the row of dropped stitch in order for stability and structure to be added to the piece that is finished. Dropped stitches can also be added as an element of design in order to make a plain project more remarkable. This is because knitting motivates one to be more imaginative in order to make knitted items that are quite unique and as such one should not hesitate to drop some stitches.

The following are some of **the uses of the dropped stitches**.

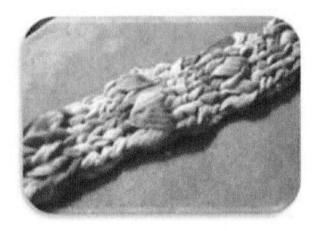

*Watch video instructions on Drop Stitch.*

# Multi-Colored Stitch

**Skill Level:** Intermediate

**Yarn:** Any

**Needle:** Straight Type

**Tools:** N/A

Multicolored knitting patterns can be applied to any piece, adding excitement and fun to the garment or product. You can combine any yarn for a variety of wonderful effects.

You can apply multicolored techniques to almost any knitting pattern to make a piece more your own, but here is an example of how you would apply it to an afghan stitch.

*Pattern Details*:

Cast on with Color A and k one row.

**Row 1 (RS)**: With Color B, p1, k1, ssk, *k9, slip 2, k1, p2sso; rep from *, end k9, k2tog, k1, slip 1 as if to k

**Row 2**: With Color B, p1, k1, *p1, k4, (k1, yo, k1) in next st, k4; rep from *, end p1, k1, slip 1 as if to k

**Rows 3 and 4**: With Color A, Rep Rows 1 and 2

Examples of multi-colored stitches include:

## Skull

**Braiding**

**Zebra**

**Multi-colored FanTail**

*More details on multi color knitting can be found here.*

# Leaf Stitches-Lace

**Skill Level:** Intermediate

**Yarn:** Any

**Needle:** Straight Type

**Tools:** N/A

The leaf pattern adds great detail to a knitted piece. Once you master this technique, you can create very intricate looking knitted pieces easily.

***Pattern Details***:

Cast on multiple of 17 stitches.

**Row 1 (Wrong Side)**: Purl across.

**Row 2 (Right Side)**: *K1, yo, k1, k2tog tbl, p1, k2tog, k1, p1, k2, p1, k2tog, k1, p1, k1; repeat from *.

**Row 3**:*P4, (k1, p2) twice, k1, p4; repeat from *.

**Row 4**: *(K1, yo) twice, (k2tog tbl, p1, k2tog), p1, (k2tog tbl, p1, k2tog), (yo, k1) twice; repeat from *.

**Row 5**:*P5, (k1, p1) twice, k1, p5; repeat from *.

**Row 6**:*K1, yo, k3, yo, sk2p, p1, k3tog, yo, k3, yo, k1; repeat from *.

**Row 7**: *P7, k1, p7; repeat from *.

**Row 8**:*K1, yo, k5, yo, sk2p, yo, k5, yo, k1; repeat from *.

*Repeat Rows 1-8 for Lace Pattern.*

# Step 1: Increase Stitches

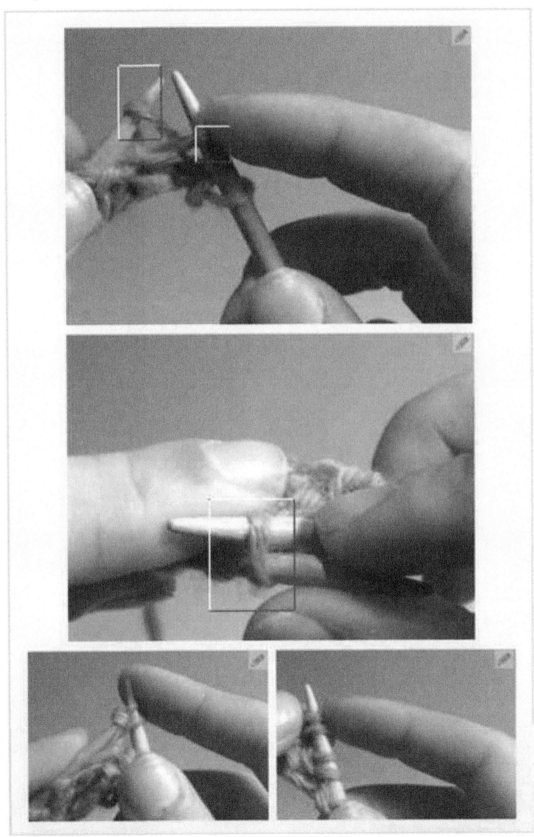

## Step 2: Increase: Yarn Over

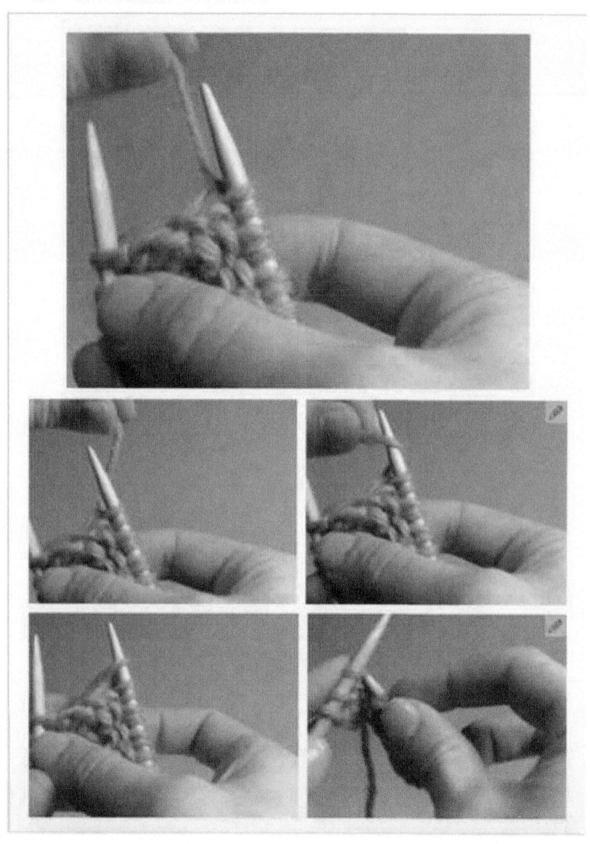

## Step 3: Decrease Stitches

## Step 4: Decrease: KRPR

# Leaves

# Spring Foliage

# Leaf fall

# Shrubs

*Watch video on* <u>*Cretan Stitch Leaf*</u>

*Watch video on* <u>*Satin Stitch Leaf*</u>

# Border & Edging Stitches

**Skill Level:** Intermediate

**Yarn:** Any

**Needle:** Straight Type

**Tools:** N/A

Edgings can be added to knitted items to finish them off in an attractive way. They can be as simplistic or as complicated as you like.

Below is the pattern for a more basic border:

*Pattern Details:*

Cast on 4 St(s)

**Row 1** - Knit

**Row 2** - Knit 2, wyif, Knit 2

**Row 3** - sl st, Knit

**Row 4** - Knit 3, wyif, Inc 1 st

**Row 5** - Knit 2, wyif, k2tog, wyif, Knit 2

**Row 6** - sl 1, Knit to end

**Row 7** – Knit 3, wyif, K2tog, wyif, Knit 2

**Row 8** – Cast off 4, Knit to end.

*Repeat these 8 rows until desired length is reached.*

## Twisting

## Border crossing

## Peacock tail

## Border with leaves

*Watch video on Shell Edging Stitch*

*Watch video on Edge/Border Stitch.*

# Rounded Patterns

**Skill Level:** Intermediate

**Yarn:** Any

**Needle:** Circular Type

**Tools:** N/A

Many knitters actually find knitting in the round easier than back and forth, because there is no right or wrong side and once you have grasped how to use circular needles, they are fantastic to work with. Round knitting is great from many different projects from hats to bags. The different effects you can create are amazing.

Circular needles are required for the rounded patterns.

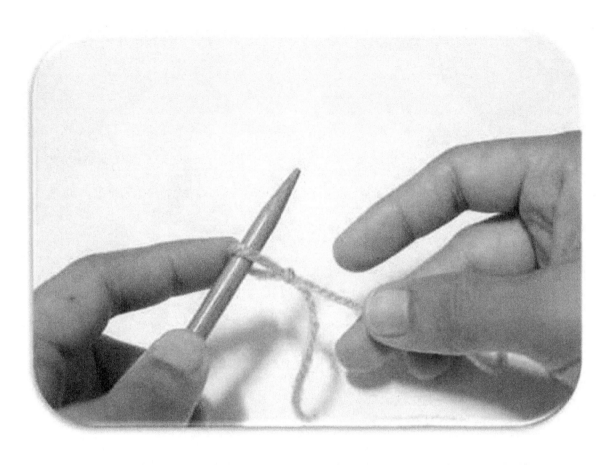

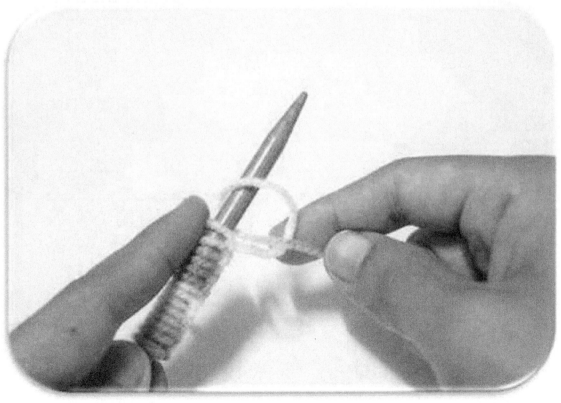

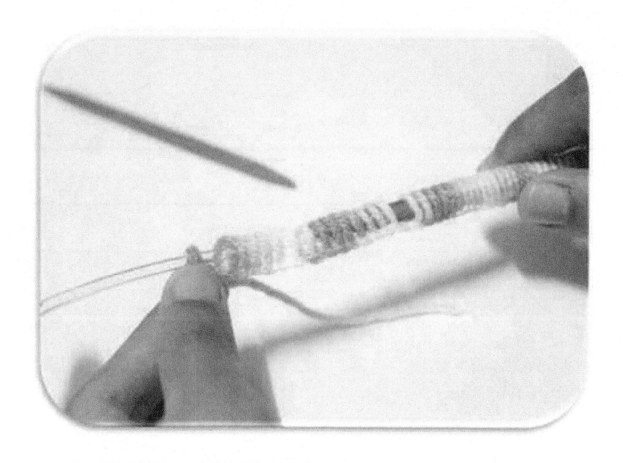

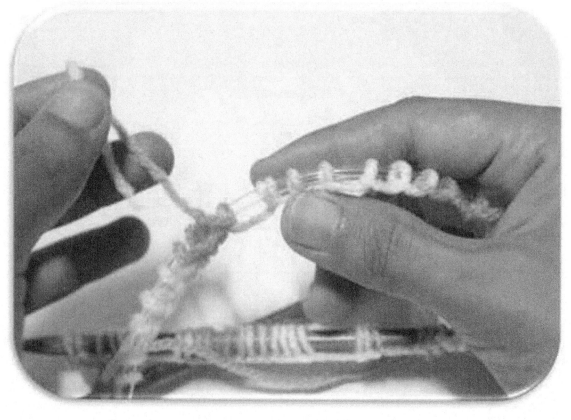

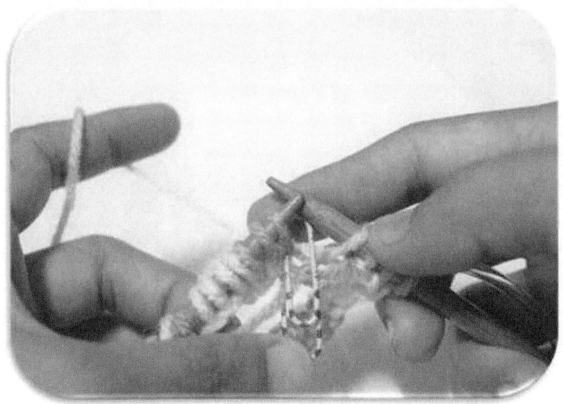

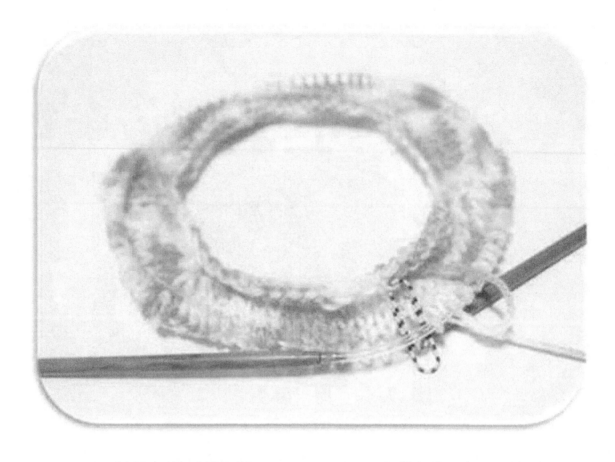

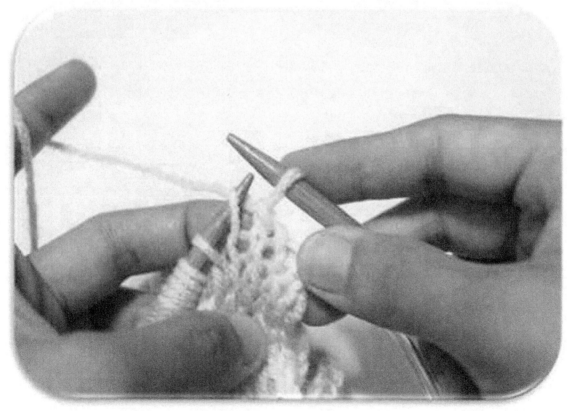

## Pattern Details

1.  You must first cast on or pick up stitches to have a foundation of stitches on your circular needles just as you would for straight knitting.

2.  Picking up the circulars so that the start of your cast-on/picked-up foundation row is in your left hand, and the end of your foundation row is in your right hand, place a marker on your right needle. This marker will indicate the end of the round. Make sure to keep your stitches untwisted!

3.  Purl or knit the first stitch on the left needle as desired. Pull the loop on the right needle through the stitch on the left needle. Pull the yarn tight to avoid a hole.

4.  Continue working the stitches. You will find that you need to periodically redistribute the stitches evenly around the circular needle so that they do not pull.

5. Continue working until you come to the marker. This marks the completion of the first round. Slip the marker to the right needle and continue working the number of rounds required.

More information on *converting stitch patterns for working in the round*.

# Geometric Patterns

**Skill Level:** Intermediate

**Yarn:** Any

**Needle:** Straight Type

**Tools:** N/A

The patterns of the slip stitch usually lend themselves quite easily to those patterns that have got sharp corners and straight lines. These patterns are at times known as *mosaic knitting* which is a term that was designed by Barbara Walker. Her thorough exploration of this technique led to further study.

A geometry pattern is as shown below.

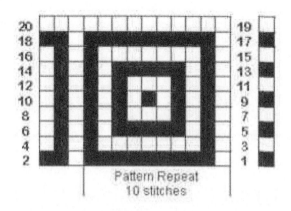

Pattern Repeat
10 stitches

*More details on* <u>*Geometric Cross Stitch pattern*</u>.

# Knit Circular or Flat

**Skill Level:** Intermediate

**Yarn:** Any

**Needle:** Straight or Circular Type

**Tools:** N/A

The slip stitch pattern can either be worked flat or circularly. The pattern that is chart for flat knitting can be converted to circular knitting by way of reading all the chart rows, the wrong side ones included just like the rows on the right side. Any edges need also to be eliminated that are called for in flat knitting in order for the pattern to repeat evenly in every round.

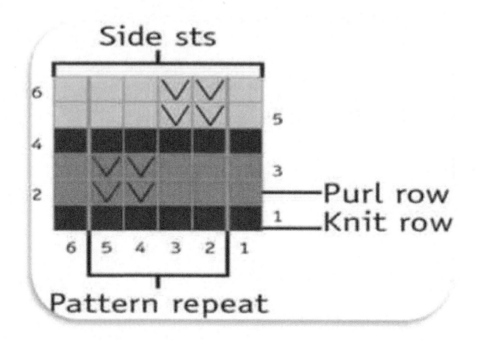

The chart for flat knitting usually calls for the edge stitches centering the pattern that repeats on the piece that is flat. The rows that are odd-numbered are knit (on the RS) while the even –numbered rows are purled on the WS.

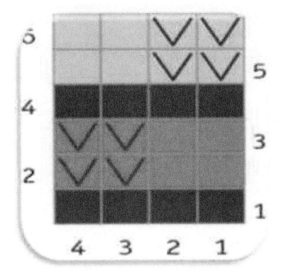

For circular knitting, the same patterns used would look as above. The edge stitches will be eliminated and all the rounds will be knit. When working in circular motion, the directions and charts need to be carefully read so that one does not forget them now that the circular knitting has got no wrong side rows.

*Video on how to* _bead flat circular Peyote stitch_

# Patterns

There are many amazing online resources for knitting patterns, as well as what will be available in your local craft shop. To get you started, here are a few patterns.

# Stitch Scarf

**Skill Level**: Beginner.

**Yarn**: 5 (Bulky)

**Needle**: Straight Type.

**Tools**: 11 or 8 mm Needles.

*Pattern Details:*

Cast on 39 stitches.

K2, p2, repeat to last 3 stitches, k2, p1.

Repeat this row. That's it!

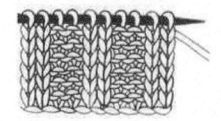

Sew in ends, wash gently by hand, block and let air dry.

*More details on How to Knit Scarf for Beginners.*

# Leaves Jacket

**Skill Level:** Intermediate.

**Yarn:** Worsted Weight.

**Needle:** Straight Type.

**Tools:** 3 mm Needles, Stitch Markers, Sewing Needle and Thread, Crochet Hook 3.

*Patterns Details:*

**Rib:** 1k, 1p

Stockinette Stitch

**1 Row** and all **odd rows** - knit sts

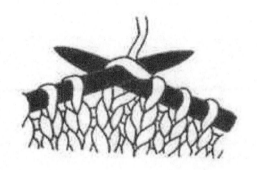

**2 Row** and all **even rows** - purl sts

Reverse Stockinette Stitch

**1 row** and all **odd rows** - purl sts

**2 row** and all **even rows** - knit sts

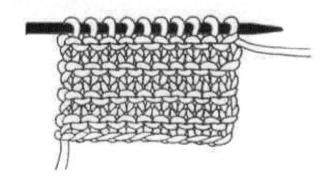

**Large Cable on 13 sts:** 1 and 3 rows - 6 k, 1 p, 6 k.

2, 4, and 6 - 6 p, 1 k, 6 p.

**Row 5** - C6B (Cable 6 Back), 1 p, C6F

Repeat rows 1-6.

**Left Leaves Panel:** on 22 st.

Row 1, 3 and 5: 10 p, 2 k, 10 p

**Row 2** and all **even rows** knit k over k, p over p and yon (yarn over needle). (If the stitch was knitted in the odd row, you purl it in the even row, if the stitch was purled in the odd row, you knit it in the even row. The yarn overs from the odd rows (starting from row 15) a to be purled.)

**Row 7**: 9 p, T2B (Twist 2 Back: slip a stitch on a cable needle and leave it at the back of work, knit next stitch, knit the stitch from the cable needle), 1 k, 10 p.

**Row 9**: 8 p, T2Bp (Twist 2 Back: slip a stitch on a cable needle and leave it at the back of work, knit next stitch, purl the stitch from the cable needle), 2 k, 10 p.

**Row 11**: 7 p, T2Bp, 1 p, 2 k, 10 p.

**Row 13**: 6 p, T2Bp, 2 p, 2 k, 10 p.

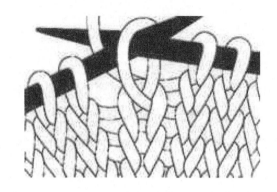

**Row 15**: 6 p, yon (yarn over needle), 1 k, yon, 3 p, 2 k, 10 p

**Row 17**: 6 p, 1 k, yon, 1 k, yon, 1 k, 3 p, 2 k, 10 p.

**Row 19**: 6 p, 2 k, yon, 1 k, yon, 2 k, 3 p, 1 k, T2F (Twist 2 Front: slip a stitch on a cable needle and leave it at the front of work, knit next stitch, knit the stitch from the cable needle), 9 p.

**Row 21**: 6 p, 3 k, yon, 1 k, yon, 3 k, 3 p, 2 k, T2Fp (Twist 2 Front: slip a stitch on a cable needle and leave it at the front of work, purl next stitch, knit the stitch from the cable needle), 8 p.

**Row 23**: 6 p, k2tog tbk (knit 2 together through back of loops), 5 k, k2tog, 3p, 2 k, 1 p, T2Fp, 7 p.

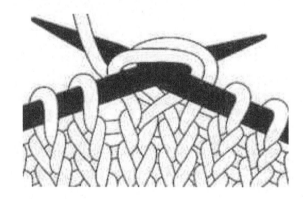

**Row 25**: 6 p, k2tog tbk, 3 k, k2tog, 3 p, 2 k, 2 p, T2Fp, 6 p.

**Row 27**: 6 p, k2tog tbk, 1 k, k2tog, 3 p, 2 k, 3 p, yon, 1 k, yon, 6 p.

**Row 29**: 6 p, sk2p (slip 1 knitwise, k2tog, psso), 3 p, 2 k, 3 p, 1 k, yon, 1 k, yon, 1 k, 6 p.

**Row 31**: 9 p, T2B, 1 k, 3 p, 2 k, yon, 1 k, yon, 2 k, 6 p.

**Row 33**: 8 p, T2Bp, 2 k, 3 p, 3 k, yon, 1 k, yon, 3 k, 6 p.

**Row 35**: 7 p, T2Bp, 1 p, 2 k, 3 p, k2tog tbk, 5 k, k2tog, 6 p.

**Row 37**: 6 p, T2Bp, 2 p, 2 k, 3 p, k2tog tbk, 3 k, k2tog, 6 p.

**Row 39**: 6 p, yon, 1 k, yon, 3 p, 2 k, 3 p, k2tog tbk, 1 k, k2tog, 6 p.

**Row 41**: 6 p, 1 k, yon, 1 k, yon, 1 k, 3 p, 2 k, 3 p, sk2p, 6 p.

**Row 43**: Repeat rows 19 - 42.

## Selvedge stitches

The 1st and last stitch of the pattern are selvedge stitches. To make the edges of your work even and smooth 2 more stitches (selvedge stitches) are added. You should always slip the first stitch as if to knit and purl the last stitch. The selvedge stitches are not counted in the pattern unless otherwise specified.

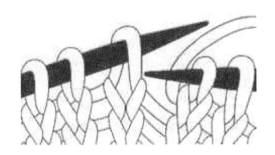

## Left Front

Cast on 53 (57, 61) sts (including edge stitches) on 3 (3.0 mm) needles.

Knit rib for 8 rows. In the last row add evenly 4 sts.

Continue on 9 (5.5 mm) needles on 57 (61, 65) sts: 1 edge st, 3 (7, 11) st. of stockinette St, 1 st of reverse stockinette st, right half of large cable on 6 st., Left Leaves panel on 22 st, large cable on 13 st, 10 st of stockinette st, 1 edge st.

Continue for 26 in. (65 cm).

To shape neckline decrease 5 st once, 3 st once, 2 st once and 1 st 5 times in each odd row.

Continue for 5 in. (12 cm). Cast off remaining 40 (44, 48) stitches.

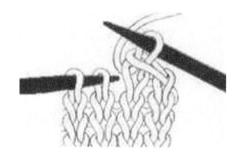

## Right Front

Knit as mirror of the left front.

## Back

Cast on 109 (113, 117) sts (including edge stitches) on 3 (3.0 mm) needles.

Knit rib for 8 rows. In the last row add evenly 5 sts.

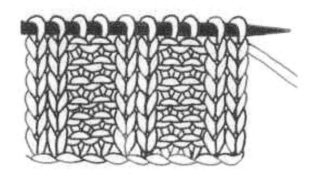

Continue on 9 (5.5 mm) needles on 114 (118, 122) sts: 1 edge st, 3 (7, 11) st. of stockinette St, 1 st of reverse stockinette st, right half of large cable on 6 st., Left Leaves panel on 22 st, large cable on 13 st, 22 st of stockinette st, large cable on 13 st, Right Leaves panel on 22 st, left half of large cable on 6 st., 1 st of reverse stockinette st, 3 (7, 11) st. of stockinette St, 1 edge st.

Continue for 29 in. (73 cm).

Cast off 22 st in the center of the back and then continue each half separately. To shape neckline decrease 3 st once, 2 st once and 1 st once in each odd row.

Continue for 1.75 in (4 cm).

Cast off remaining 40 (44, 48) st on both sides.

Sleeve:

Cast on 43 sts (including edge stitches) on 3 (3.0 mm) needles.

Knit rib for 8 rows. In the last row add evenly 25 (29, 33) sts.

Continue stockinette stitch on 9 (5.5 mm) needles.

Add on both sides 1 st 18 times in each 4th row - 104 (108, 112) sts.

Continue for 16 in (40 cm). cast off.

## Finishing:

Crochet button bands with sc (single crochet) for 1 in (2.5 cm). On the right band make 7 buttonholes.

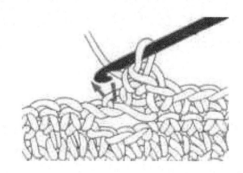

Join shoulder seams. Pick up 139 st on 3 (3.0 mm) needles along the neckline and knit rib for 10 rows. Cast off.

Sew in sleeves. Join side seams. Sew on 7 buttons.

*Watch video on* <u>*Leaf Motif Jacket*</u>

# Snowy Owl

**Skill Level**: Advanced.

**Yarn**: Bulky.

**Needle**: Circular Type, Double Pointed Type.

**Tools**: Stuffing.

*Pattern Details:*

**Round 1**: Knit into the front and back (kfb) 8 times. (16 stitches)

**Round 2:** Purl.

**Round 3**: *P1, kfb, repeat from * to end of round. (24 stitches)

**Round 4:** Purl.

**Round 5**: *P2, kfb, repeat from * to end of round. (32 stitches)

**Round 6:** Purl.

**Round 7:** *P3, kfb, repeat from * to end of round. (40 stitches)

**Round 8:** Purl.

**Round 9:** *P4, kfb, repeat from * to end of round. (48 stitches)

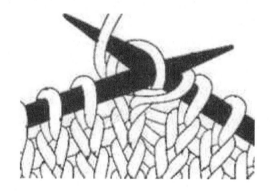

**Round 10**: Purl.

**Round 11**: *P5, kfb, repeat from * to end of round. (56 stitches).

Switching to the 20 inch circular needle.

**Round 12**: Purl.

**Round 13**: *P13, kfb, repeat from * to end of round. (60 stitches)

Purl 6 rounds.

## The Body

**Round 1**: *P1, k9, p1, k1, repeat from * to end of round.

**Round 2**: *K1, p1, k7, p1, k1, p1, repeat from * to end of round.

**Round 3**: *P1, k1, p1, k5, (p1, k1) 2 times, repeat from * to end of round.

**Round 4:** *(K1, p1) 2 times, k3, p1, k1, p1, k2, repeat from * to end of round.

**Round 5:** *K2, (p1, k1) 3 times, p1, k3, repeat from * to end of round.

**Round 6:** *K3, (p1, k1) 2 times, p1, k4, repeat from * to end of round.

**Round 7:** *K4, p1, k1, p1, k5, repeat from * to end of round.

**Round 8:** Repeat Round 6.

**Round 9:** Repeat Round 5.

**Round 10**: Repeat Round 4.

**Round 11:** Repeat Round 3.

**Round 12:** Repeat Round 2.

Repeat Rounds 1-12 one more time.

Repeat Rounds 1-7.

## The Head

**Rounds 1-6**: Knit.

**Round 7:** *K8, k2tog, repeat from * to end of round. (54 stitches)

**Rounds 8 and 9**: Knit.

**Round 10**: *K7, k2tog, repeat from * to end of round. (48 stitches)

**Rounds 11 and 12**: Knit.

**Round 13**: *K6, k2tog, repeat from * to end of round. (42 stitches)

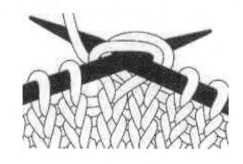

**Rounds 14 and 15**: Knit.

**Round 16**: *K5, k2tog, repeat from * to end of round. (36 stitches)

**Rounds 17 and 18**: Knit.

Turn the piece inside out and weave in the ends. Then turn it right side out and fill the owl with a bag of stuffing.


## The Ears

Remove the stitch marker, and slip the last 5 stitches you knit onto a double pointed needle.

With a second double pointed needle, knit the next 5 stitches.

Rearrange these 10 stitches onto three double pointed needles (3 stitches on two and 4 stitches on the third). Join for working in the round.

**\*\*Rounds 1-3**: Knit.

**Round 4**: (K3, k2tog) 2 times. (8 stitches)

**Round 5:** (K2, k2tog) 2 times. (6 stitches)

**Round 6:** (K1, k2tog) 2 times. (4 stitches)

Cut the yarn and sew it through the remaining stitches.\*\*\*

Orient your owl so the ear you just made is on the right (as in the above picture). Use the back circular needle to slip 8 stitches from the front needle.

Slip the next 10 stitches onto three double pointed needles (3 stitches on two and 4 stitches on the third). Join new yarn, and repeat from ** to ***, joining into the round at the beginning of the second round.

Finish stuffing your owl, making it firm and plump. Don't forget to stuff the ears too!

Separate the 16 remaining stitches so that there are 8 stitches at each end of the needle.

Cut a piece of the Main Yarn about 24 inches long. Thread it onto a tapestry needle and graft the two sides of the owl's head together using the Kitchener Stitch.

As you weave in the tails, sew closed the holes.


## The Eyes

With Color A, cast 8 stitches onto the double pointed needles.

Join for working in the round, being careful to not twist the stitches.

**Round 1**: Kfb 8 times. (16 stitches)

**Round 2**: *K1, kfb, repeat from * to end of round. (24 stitches)

Change to Color B.

**Round 3**: Knit.

**Round 4**: *K2, kfb, repeat from * to end of round. (32 stitches)

Change to Color C.

**Round 5**: Knit.

**Round 6**: *K3, kfb, repeat from * to end of round. (40 stitches)

Bind off, leaving a 24 inch tail. Weave in all the ends, except the tail. Use the tail to close the circle.

Make another eye identical to the first.

Place the edge of one eye half way between the ears and down at the center of the head. Use the tail to sew the outside edge of the eye to the head. To do this, I sewed under a ladder stitch of the head then up through a bind off stitch and down through the adjacent bind off stitch, ready to sew under the next ladder stitch.

Sew the second eye down also, lining up the outside edge so that the two eyes meet in the middle of the head.

Cut a 30 inch piece of Color D and thread it onto a tapestry needle. Embroider around the inside of the first eye by bringing the needle down through the center of the eye and up through the first round of knitting, then back down through the center until you have gone all the way around the center of the eye. Weave in the ends.

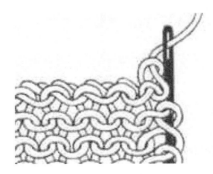

Embroider around the second eye in the same way.

## The Beak

With Color D and a double pointed needle, pick up 6 stitches along the inside curve of the owl's left eye.

Flip the owl upside down, and with a second double pointed needle, pick up 6 stitches down the inside of the right eye. (12 stitches)

For the beak, you'll work back and forth in rows, working across the first double pointed needle and then the second. Turn the work over between rows.

**Row 1**: Purl.

**Row 2**: K3, k2tog, k2, ssk, k3. (10 stitches)

**Row 3**: Purl.

**Row 4**: K2, k2tog, k2, ssk, k2. (8 stitches)

Now, with 4 stitches on each needle, cut the yarn, leaving an 18 inch tail.

Hold the two needles parallel to each other, and graft them together using the Kitchener Stitch.

Weave in the ends.

If you have any ends left over, weave them in.

*Watch video on _how to knit an owl_.*

# Common Mistakes in Knitting

## Dropping a Stitch

Dropping a stitch is an easy mistake to make, and you'll notice it because your piece will have a tear or a wayward stitch at the bottom. As soon as you realize what you have done, it's best to put a locking stitch marker on it so that it doesn't untangle further.

To recover the stitch you'll want to reach through the dropped stitch with a crochet hook, and pick up the bottommost strand in the ladder. Then, pull the strand through the stitch towards you to form a new stitch.

*Watch video on how to pick up a Dropped Stitch*

# Too Many Stitches

Often new knitters will accidently knit too many stitches at the beginning of a row, which will become obvious as the piece will look clumpy and uneven. You can either fix this by unraveling the work you have done, redistribute the yarn or decrease it later. This last option works best if it's on a seam.

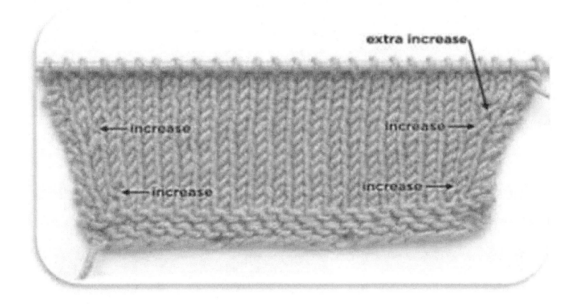

Among the stitches adjacent, redistribute extra yarn from every stitch that you undo. The increased stitch should be dropped off the needle.

The excess yarn is then pulled off by use of a tapestry needle to the stitches adjacent so that the extra yarn will not be noticed.

Now use a tapestry needle that the yarn could be redistributed among adjacent stitches.

*Watch video on how to avoid extra knit stitches.*

# Tight Knitting

Tight knitting can occur as a result of pulling your yarn and gripping the needles. Consequently, the needles become very tight such that you can hardly get stitches right through your needles. If the tightness is uncomfortable, ensure that a few rows are ripped out and reworked. As soon as is noticeable, the missed increase can be compensated for.

The best manner to prevent the mistakes from happening is:

Keep admiring your work more often so that in case something begins to look not right, you first stop to investigate. You may have accidentally done over a yarn or you may have been knitting on the needle's tips. Just like it is the case with unusual rashes, when you ignore the knitting problems, you may not have solved the problem. Therefore, you need to be very vigilant.

The easiest way to fix mistakes is to not make them in the first place, and the second-easiest way is to find them shortly after you made them.

Figuratively, look at the progress of your work every few number of rows or even when you are just about to start shaping. Scrutinize if the row increase is mirrored in case the piece should assume symmetry. Find out if the count in stitch is correct and whether the fabric looks like what you are expecting. Measure the gauge and ensure that it matches with a swatch. Early checking in your work ensures that most mistakes are discovered in time.

# FAQ

## 1. How do I close stitch when knitting?

To finish off a knitting project, you'll need to:

- **Cast Off** – knit the first two stitches from the left needle onto the right needle, then push the tip of the left needle into the first stitch on the right needle.

- **Drop Off** – lift the first stitch over the second stitch and drop it off the right needle. Knit another stitch from the left needle and do the same again. Continue in the same way until there are no stitches on the left needle and just one stitch on the right needle.

- **Cut** – cut the yarn, leaving a 6-inch end. With your fingers, gently pull on the last stitch to make it a little bit bigger, then take the needle out and pull the end of the yarn all the way through the loop, take the needle out and pull the yarn tight.

- **Crochet Hook** – hold the needle in your left hand and pick up the crochet hook with your right hand. Slip the first stitch onto the hook, then insert the hook into the next stitch, catch the yarn, and pull it through both stitches.

- **Cut** – cut the yarn with some scissors, then catch the yarn end and pull it through the last loop.

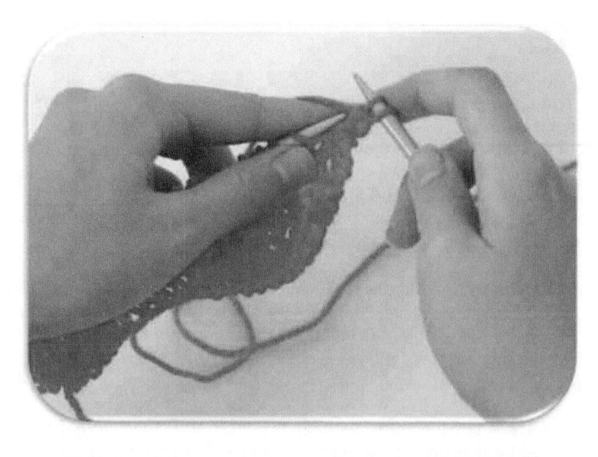

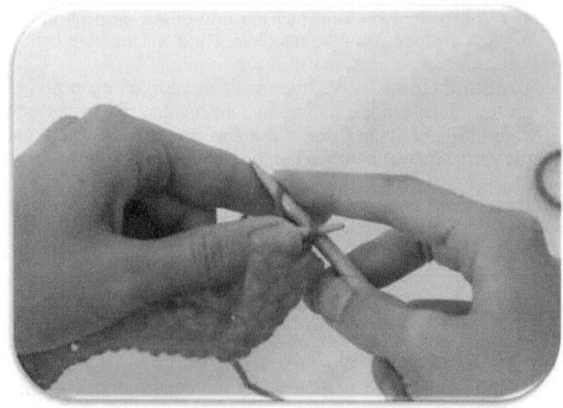

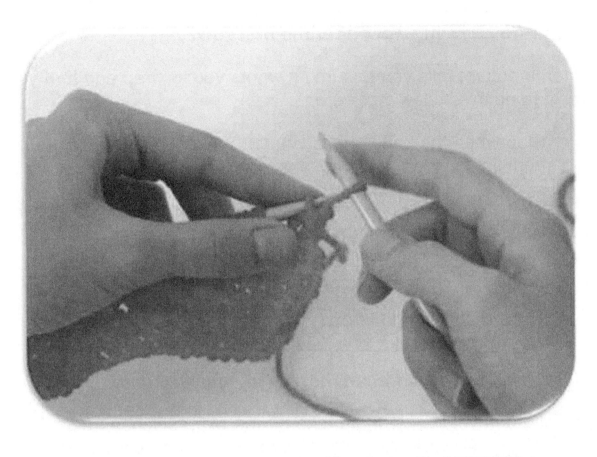

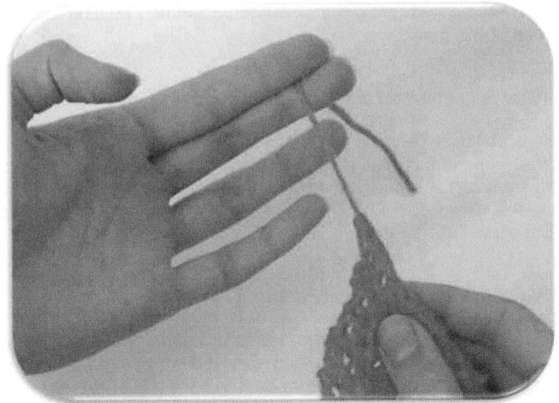

## 2. How do I turn my work after the first row?

When a pattern tells you to 'turn', it wants you to wrap and turn your work. To do this, follow these steps:

- Stop when the pattern tells you to 'turn' and slip the next stitch from the left to the right needle.

- Bring the working yarn to the front of your work, then slip the stitch back from the right to the left needle.

- Move the working yarn to the back of the work again.

- Turn your work around.

## 3. How do I fix the extra stitches on my needle?

You can unravel your work to take off the extra stitches, redistribute the yarn or decrease the stitches later. This is a common mistake that is very easily fixable. Check out the 'Common Knitting Mistakes' section of this guide.

## 4. What is the correct way to wrap the yarn on my needle?

This is obviously a technique that you will develop a preference for as you work, but as a starting point it's a good idea to wrap the yarn from front to back on the needle and steady it using your fingers. Use the 'Yarn for Beginners' section in this guide for more information.

## 5. Why are there holes in my knitting?

This is a common for beginners. Holes are often caused by uneven tension or by inadvertently making yarn overs in your work, so just remember to move your yarn from front to back as you work.

*Watch video on fixing common mistakes in knitting.*

# Conclusion

So as this guide has demonstrated, knitting is a fun, useful skill that isn't too hard to master. Once you have mastered all of the stitches and tips, you can go on to create unique and amazing things. In today's high speed world, knitting is a relaxing hobby which is as calming as it is productive.

Aside from the health benefits of knitting, it's also a very cost effective hobby. Patterns are cheap (or free) and all knitting equipment can be purchased on a budget. Once you have gotten to grip with the basics of knitting, you'll be in a position to create your very own patterns – saving you even more money.

There are many amazing resources online for knitters – in fact, there is quite a huge community of web pages and forums where users can share their tips and tricks. This is a great way to discover ore about your new skill, whilst meeting new people from all over the world and making friends. Once you have the ability to knitting, you won't look back!

Printed in Great Britain
by Amazon